Thomas W. Leonhardt, MLS
Editor

Handbook of Electronic and Digital Acquisitions

"With the *Handbook of Electronic and Digital Acquisitions,* Thomas W. Leonhardt has compiled a resource that ranges from the general to the specific, that offers sound advice and perspective for the novice as well as the veteran, and that bears not only on collections but also on technical services and reference. For the librarian new to the mysteries of digital collections, Van Kampen surveys the important legislation that informs the access to and use of the broad spectrum of electronic resources. For the mid-career librarian who finds that the acquisitions of electronic resources has taken on a life of its own, that the decision-making process has gotten more opportunistic than methodical, Powers describes a thoughtful, objective process for assessing the merit and use of electronic databases. Evaluation criteria, statistical measures, and sample forms are provided. For those of us who have been in the trenches a while now but sometimes wonder how we got to this point, McMullen and her co-authors provide a useful historical review and offer some perspective on the need for and content of collection development policies for electronic resources.

If your library is implementing electronic reserves, I recommend the chapter by Linda Neyer. She takes a deep, detailed look into copyright law and the fair use provisions. She provides an extensive checklist of factors to consider by librarians who wish to establish new or revise existing guidelines and procedures for electronic reserves.

Many technical services librarians have hitched their processing wagons to materials vendors' online systems. Zhang and Williams summarize the integration of library acquisitions functions with materials vendors' online systems, ILS functionality, and bibliographic utilities. While standards and routines have been established and many efficiencies gained, a strict interdependence of the parties has resulted. As standards change will these connections remain?

The *Handbook of Electronic and Digital Acquisitions* extends its range and narrows its scope to offer insight into the different levels of functionality of virtual reference software. Slater and Johnson provide the facts and pose the questions that will allow librarians to decide the kind of VR service they wish to provide their users."

Richard Brumley, MLS
Head of Collection Development,
Oregon State University Libraries

Handbook of Electronic and Digital Acquisitions

THE HAWORTH PRESS
New, Recent, and Forthcoming
Titles of Related Interest

Acquisitions and Collection Development in the Humanities edited by Irene Owens

Collection Management and Strategic Access to Digital Resources: The New Challenges for Research Libraries edited by Sul H. Lee

Digital versus Non-Digital Reference: Ask a Librarian Online and Offline edited by Jessamyn West

Electronic Collection Management edited by Suzanne D. McGinnis

Integrating Print and Digital Resources in Library Collections edited by Audrey Fenner

The Internet and Acquisitions: Sources and Resources for Development edited by Mary E. Timmons

Managing Digital Resources in Libraries edited by Audrey Fenner

Research Collections and Digital Information edited by Sul H. Lee

Handbook of Electronic and Digital Acquisitions

Thomas W. Leonhardt, MLS
Editor

The Haworth Press
New York • London • Oxford

For more information on this book or to order, visit
http://www.haworthpress.com/store/product.asp?sku=5580

or call 1-800-HAWORTH (800-429-6784) in the United States and Canada
or (607) 722-5857 outside the United States and Canada

or contact orders@HaworthPress.com

Published by

The Haworth Press, Inc., 10 Alice Street, Binghamton, NY 13904-1580.

PUBLISHER'S NOTES
The development, preparation, and publication of this work has been undertaken with great care. However, the Publisher, employees, editors, and agents of The Haworth Press are not responsible for any errors contained herein or for consequences that may ensue from use of materials or information contained in this work. The Haworth Press is committed to the dissemination of ideas and information according to the highest standards of intellectual freedom and the free exchange of ideas. Statements made and opinions expressed in this publication do not necessarily reflect the views of the Publisher, Directors, management, or staff of The Haworth Press, Inc., or an endorsement by them.

Due to the ever-changing nature of the Internet, Web site names and addresses, although verified to the best of the publisher's ability, should not be accepted as accurate without independent verification.

Cover design by Lora Wiggins.

Library of Congress Cataloging-in-Publication Data

Handbook of electronic and digital acquisitions / Thomas W. Leonhardt, editor.
    p. cm.
Includes bibliographical references and index.
ISBN-13: 978-0-7890-2291-2 (alk. paper)
ISBN-10: 0-7890-2291-5 (alk. paper)
ISBN-13: 978-0-7890-2292-9 (pbk. : alk. paper)
ISBN-10: 0-7890-2292-3 (pbk. : alk. paper)
    1. Libraries—Special collections—Electronic information resources. 2. Acquisition of electronic information resources. 3. Database selection. 4. Copyright—Electronic information resources—United States. 5. Electronic information resources—Fair use (Copyright)—United States. 6. Electronic reserve collections in libraries—Law and legislation. 7. Electronic reference services (Libraries)—Computer programs. 8. Acquisitions (Libraries)—Automation. 9. Collection development (Libraries). 10. Digital libraries—Collection development. I. Leonhardt, Thomas W.

Z692.C65H348 2006
025.2'84—dc22

              2005024826

CONTENTS

ABOUT THE EDITOR

Thomas W. Leonhardt, MLS, is Director of the Scarborough-Phillips Library at St. Edward's University in Austin, Texas. He has been an academic librarian for more than 30 years and has worked in acquisitions, technical services, and library administration in public and private institutions. Leonhardt is a regular columnist for *Against the Grain and Technicalities,* and has edited several books and periodicals. He is past President of LITA (the Library and Information Technology Association).

doi:10.1300/5580_a

Contributors

Rickey D. Best, MLIS, MA, is Dean of the Auburn University at Montgomery Library. Mr. Best received his MLIS from the University of California–Berkeley and his MA in history from the University of California–Riverside. He has been published in *College and Research Libraries News; Library Collections, Acquisitions, and Technical Services;* and the *Journal of San Diego History.*

Patricia B. M. Brennan, MSLS, is Assistant Professor/Head of Reference and Coordinator of Library Instruction at the James P. Adams Library, Rhode Island College, Providence, Rhode Island. Professor Brennan received her MSLS from Columbia University. Her current areas of research interest include open access to and open archiving of scholarly information as well as the response of the academy to issues surrounding academic honesty. Her most recent article, "The Truth About Plagiarism," appeared in *Issues in Teaching and Learning,* 1(1), 2002.

Joanna M. Burkhardt, MLS, is Associate Professor/Head Librarian at the University of Rhode Island–Providence Campus Library. Professor Burkhardt received her MLS from the University of Rhode Island, Kingston. Her current areas of research interest include student learning assessment, information literacy, and teaching methods. She is co-author (with Mary C. MacDonald and Andree J. Rathemacher) of *Teaching in College Libraries: 35 Practical Standards-Based Exercises for College Students* (Chicago: American Library Association, 2003), and a forthcoming volume, *Creating a Comprehensive Information Literacy Plan: A How-To-Do-It Manual and CD-ROM for Libraries* (New York: Neal Shuman, 2005).

Denise Johnson, MSLS, is Reference/Government Documents Librarian and Library Liaison to the Foster College of Business,

doi:10.1300/5580_b

Cullom-Davis Library, Bradley University, Peoria, Illinois. Ms. Johnson received her MS in library science from the University of Illinois at Urbana/Champaign. She is a regular reviewer for *Library Journal* and *Business Information Alert,* has contributed chapters to several books, including *Local and Regional Government Information,* Mary Martin, ed. (Westport, CT: Greenwood Press, 2005), and *Managing Business Collections in Libraries,* Carolyn Sheehy, ed. (Westport, CT: Greenwood Press, 1996), and was a co-editor of and a contributor to *Patron Behavior in Libraries* (Chicago: ALA Editions, 1996). Ms. Johnson is a governing board member of the MyWeb Librarian.com collaborative virtual reference service.

Susan McMullen, MLS, MS, is Associate Professor/Information Resources Librarian, Roger Williams University Library, Bristol, Rhode Island. Ms. McMullen received her MLS in library science from the State University of New York at Geneseo and her MS in information resource management from Syracuse University. Her specialty research areas include library Web site usability and information-seeking behaviors of online users. She has been published in *Reference Services Review* and the *Journal of Government Information.*

Linda Neyer, MLS, is Reference Librarian, Database Coordinator, and Subject Specialist for Science and Health Sciences at the Andruss Library, Bloomsburg University, Bloomsburg, Pennsylvania. She received her MLS from University at Albany, State University of New York, in Albany, New York. Her research interests include studying information use behaviors in the science and health science disciplines and improving library accessibility to students with physical and learning disabilities.

Audrey Powers, MLS, is Research Librarian for the Sciences and Technology at the University of South Florida, Tampa Library, Tampa, Florida. Her research areas include genetics, medicine, physics, computer science, and engineering. She is the column editor of *Snapshot Reviews* in *The Charleston Advisor.*

Robert Slater, MA, is Digital Information Services Librarian at the Kresge Library, Oakland University, Rochester, Michigan. Mr. Slater received his MA in library and information science from the University of Illinois in Urbana, Illinois. His research is focused on

Internet-delivered library resources and services. He has been published in *Science & Technology Libraries.*

Doris Van Kampen, EdD, is Systems Librarian and holds the rank of Assistant Professor in the Cannon Memorial Library at Saint Leo University, Saint Leo, Florida. Dr. Van Kampen received her EdD in curriculum and instruction from the University of Central Florida in Orlando, Florida, and her LIS from the University of South Florida. Her specialty research areas include the information search process and information-seeking behavior, with a focus on graduate students, engineers, and historians; information retrieval; copyright and intellectual property; and young adult and children's literature written in the 1950s, 1960s, and 1970s. She has been published in *College & Research Libraries, Journal of Library and Information Services in Distance Learning, Women in Higher Education Newsletter,* and *Florida Media Quarterly.*

Marla Wallace, MLS, is Coordinator of Reference and Collection Development at the Community College of Rhode Island–Flanagan Campus Library, Lincoln, Rhode Island. Professor Wallace received her BA and MLS from the University of Wisconsin–Madison. She is active in promoting information literacy at the college and was instrumental in designing a one-credit course taught by librarians, "Introduction to Library Research on the Internet."

John H. Williams, BA, has been Acquisitions Manager at Wichita State University Libraries since 1996. He has had articles published in *Scott's Stamp Monthly, Serials Review,* and *Library Collections,* and *Acquisitions and Technical Services,* and is co-author of *Current Essays and Reports in Information Retrieval and Data Mining: An Annotated Bibliography of Shorter Monographs* (Lanham, MD: Scarecrow Press, 2005). He was a Russian linguist working for the Army Security Agency during the Vietnam War attached to both the Naval Security Group and the Air Force Security Service. He is currently working on a book concerning Calvin Mooers.

Sha Li Zhang, PhD, has been Assistant Director for Technical Services at the University of North Carolina Greensboro Libraries since March 2005. Prior to that, she was Head of Technical Services at Wichita State University Libraries from 1999 to 2005. She has been very active in serving on committees of the American Library

Association (ALA), the Association of College and Research Libraries (ACRL), the Association for Library Collections and Technical Services (ALCTS), the International Relations Round Table (IRRT), and regional and state library associations. Zhang was elected ALA Councilor-at-Large in 2004 for a three-year term. She has published articles in *College & Research Libraries, Library Collections, Acquisitions, and Technical Services; Library Trends;* and *Journal of China Society for Library Science.*

Preface

When I was in the army, we had a saying: "There's the right way, the wrong way, and the army way." In libraries, we follow the same philosophy, and, even if we don't say it, there is a right way, a wrong way, and my library way of doing things. Even when applying cataloging rules and standards, each library has its own interpretations for meeting local needs, and each library tends to look to others.

The same is true in the current electronic and digital environment. Standards abound, but local issues, concerns, and environments differ, almost guaranteeing that, within common frameworks, we all do things just a little bit differently than our colleagues.

But librarians do not like reinventing the wheel, either, so they attend conferences and workshops and subscribe to LISTSERV and still use the telephone to contact colleagues when in doubt about something. We also write about our experiences and publish them as scholarly articles and case studies.

Handbook of Electronic and Digital Acquisitions combines scholarly approaches with case studies and practical questions to ask when, for example, you are evaluating databases that you may want to subscribe to along with databases that you are using. In the first two chapters, Van Kampen and Neyer take broad, practical looks at copyright as it applies to the Technology, Education, and Copyright Harmonization Act, Digital Millennium Copyright Act, fair use guidelines and policies, Association of Research Libraries statements about electronic reserves, off-site and in-house database use issues, and so on. Their subject, covered in two chapters, provides overviews of the law and gives practical suggestions about how to make it all work for your library.

Audrey Powers, Susan McMullen et al., and Rickey D. Best are interested in how to evaluate online databases and aggregated sources of material from various publishers. Best takes a historical approach to evaluation using the Western Library Network/Association of Research Libraries conspectus. The others offer templates and questions

doi:10.1300/5580_c

to be asked when looking at databases for purchase or retention. All three approaches are flexible and are not restricted to any one type of library.

Students living on campus and studying or writing papers inside the library want online resources, but virtual reference services are particularly important to distance-learning students because, when they have a problem using a database, they cannot walk up to a reference librarian and get help. A virtual reference service is one way to provide help for these students, but not all products are equal. Robert Slater and Denise Johnson give detailed, practical information about products on the market and how to choose the right one for your needs. They also include a helpful glossary to ensure that you understand how they are using terms.

Zhang and Williams offer information about the electronic transfer of acquisitions and bibliographic data between libraries and vendors. They provide an environmental scan of standards and practices relating to data transfer and include screen displays to illustrate their points.

We offer this handbook in the spirit of sharing and hope that it helps you find new approaches to what you do or that it confirms your own practices and experiences.

Chapter 1

Acquisitions and Copyright

Doris Van Kampen

INTRODUCTION

Your institution made the decision to lease a database or buy an electronic resource. Now that you have one, how are you legally allowed to use it? One perspective is that you have paid for it, so, like a book, you can lend it, copy from it, put some of it on reserve, and allow access to it online. Other perspectives are not as inclusive.

Copyright is like a roughly outlined canvas waiting for an artist with a many-colored palette to apply the right mixture of paint and dedication in order to complete a masterpiece. Why? Because copyright is an issue with many colors, perspectives, and interpretations, depending on whether you are the copyright owner, the information broker, the reproduction rights organization, the library, or the user. The endeavor to clarify and understand this murkiest of issues will continue long after this book has been printed. I cannot answer all the questions that may arise when reading this chapter, but I can raise the awareness that questions do, indeed, need to be asked.

Electronic resources continue to consume larger and larger portions of a library's budget. This has become a long-term trend, with more money being spent on electronic resources and more restrictions being added by vendors and by legislation. Many libraries are beginning to realize that a close look needs to be taken at these issues and at their licensing agreements. Any libraries that have not yet formalized their guidelines for purchasing, leasing, and using electronic resources would be wise to do so.

doi:10.1300/5580_01

STATISTICS ON EXPENDITURES
FOR ELECTRONIC RESOURCES

1999-2000, Association of Research Libraries

- Electronic Resources account for 12.9 percent of the library materials budget.
- 105 ARL libraries reported spending almost $100 million on electronic resources.
- 38 ARL libraries reported a total of $9.5 million in additional funds spent through a centrally funded consortium for purchasing electronic products and services.

2000-2001, Association of Research Libraries

- Electronic Resources account for 16.25 percent, on average, of the library materials budget.
- $132 million is spent on electronic resources.
- $14.66 million in additional funds is spent through a consortium for purchasing electronic products and services.
- Expenditures for electronic serials increased by 75 percent between 1999 and 2001 alone, and almost 900 percent since they were first reported, in 1994-1995.

2001-2002, Association of Research Libraries

- Electronic resources account for 19.60 percent on average of the library materials budget.
- 108 ARL libraries report spending $16.7 million for ebooks.
- 108 ARL libraries report spending $154.4 million on electronic serials.
- 43 ARL libraries spent $53.5 million for full-text ejournals.[1]

Information and access to it are big concerns to all the interested parties. The aggregator wants to make a profit. The originator wants to receive fees for agreeing to provide his or her work. Some factors to consider when making leasing and purchasing decisions include the following:

1. Copyright, access, and fair use: in-house use, off-site use, and distance learning
2. Licensing agreements: reserves and course packs as part of the agreement
3. Interlibrary loan of licensed and leased materials
4. Overlapping resources

These decisions will have a major impact on what you can do with the materials once you own or lease them.

All of the possible users of copyrighted materials need to be considered, and open discussions need to be held with all of the stakeholders at the institution, including the campus information technology (IT) department, the copyright officer, and all of the library departments. Why should the campus IT department be included in the discussions? The campus IT or academic computing department's decisions affect how the library accesses the Internet. Furthermore, the campus IT department has licensing agreements with courseware vendors, such as Blackboard and WebCT. Each of these licenses and how the institution's Internet access is set up may affect (at least to some degree) what types of linking instructors can do within the courseware and which systems and databases the library decides to buy.

Libraries exist to serve recreational, educational, and other informational needs by managing, disseminating, and allowing access to information. Access includes the library's Web site, individual user authentication, institutional Internet protocol (IP) authentication, print and electronic interlibrary loan, print and electronic document delivery, e-mail, online request forms, and patron privacy issues.

Before deciding whether to purchase an item, lease a database, or provide electronic reserves and reference services you must consider copyright laws and licensing agreements. Copyright laws exist to protect authors' and inventors' rights by balancing the rights of the creator(s) to limit access and the rights of the public to have access. The goal of your database provider will be to define the rights as narrowly as possible so that the maximum amount of revenue can be obtained. The goal of the library should be to define the license as broadly as possible in order to increase the leverage of the library's budget and to protect the patrons' right to free access to information.

COPYRIGHT 101

The patent and copyright clause of the U.S. Constitution, Article I, Section 8, Clause 8 states that Congress shall have the power "to promote the progress of science and useful arts, by securing for limited times to authors and inventors the exclusive right to their respective writings and discoveries."

Title 17, Section 108 of the U.S. Code allows a library to make a single copy of an article upon request for interlibrary loan without violating copyright, if the following conditions are met by the library:

- The library is open to the public.
- Copying is done without any direct or indirect commercial advantage.
- No systematic or multiple copying is permitted, and copies must be given to the patron.
- Item(s) copied are owned by the library.
- The number of items requested from any one work is limited to five per calendar year, barring a few exceptions, with one of the exceptions being the age of the item requested.

Section 109 of the copyright law allows an owner of a particular work to sell, lend, rent, lease, or give away an item that has been purchased. "Once the copyright owner agrees to sell a particular copy of a work, the copyright owner may not control further. . . ."[2] However, Section 109 was written long before there were electronic resources licensing agreements, computers, and digital conundrums. It may apply only to items that have been bought, not leased or shared within a consortium, depending on how the courts rule. If the first sale doctrine is not able to be applied to digital items, there may well be a shortage of materials available for interlibrary loan and document delivery in the near future, especially if either one of the two bills (Consumer Access to information Act of 2004, HR 3872, and Database and Collections of Information Misappropriation Act, HR 3261) under review as of March 2004 by the House Energy and Commerce and Judiciary Committees is passed.

The Consumer Access to Information Act of 2004 (HR 3872) is designed "to prohibit the misappropriation of databases while ensuring consumer access to factual information. . . . [It emphasizes the] importance of databases to commerce"[3] while purportedly opposing the creation of additional "protection for factual information when harm has not been demonstrated and there exist a number of federal and state remedies to protect databases."[4] The committee states that HR 3872 codifies the Supreme Court decision in *INS v. AP*, 248 U.S. 215 (1918) and by the 2nd Circuit Court of Appeals decision in *NBA v. Motorola*, 105 F.3d 841 (2nd Cir. 1997).

The Database and Collections of Information Misappropriation Act (HR 3261) is designed "to prohibit the misappropriation of certain databases. . . . [It] makes civilly liable any person who makes available in commerce to others a substantial part of the information contained in a database generated, gathered, or maintained by another person without authorization."[5]

FAIR USE

Fair use limits a copyright owner's exclusive right to his or her work "for purposes such as criticism, comment, news reporting, teaching (including multiple copies for classroom use), scholarship, or research."[6] It is designed to protect the rights of the end user, which is not usually the library, but the patron. The library may order materials for a patron, and it may send materials to another institution, but the library is not the one that will eventually be publishing information based on the materials ordered. The patron for whom the material was ordered will be using the information. The library simply provides access.

As society changed from an industrial, goods-based economy to an information- and consumer-based society, tension among copyright owners, for-profit information providers, and libraries grew. The fair use clause of federal copyright law is not always perceived to be in the best interest of business; indeed, it is often viewed as a threat. HR 3261, if passed, "would fundamentally allow database producers to lock up facts through copyright-like law."[7] Until the advent of Napster and other file-sharing programs, however, academic uses remained a sacrosanct right. "Throughout the language of copyright law and related court cases, one assumption is unchallenged and pervasive: education, and by extension academic research, is a public good."[8] Development of policies and procedures for licensing, delivering, borrowing, ending, managing, and archiving digital materials that comply with copyright laws yet protect the rights of the user to have fair and equitable access has become imperative. Libraries need to persist in defending the rights of users to access information while balancing their rights with those of the authors, publishers, and copyright owners of digital information. Having sound acquisitions policies and procedures in place is critical because they will influence licensing agreement negotiations.

How is the idea of fair use changing? "The software industry is working hard to eliminate for digital content the built-in exemptions libraries enjoy under existing copyright laws—exemptions that allow them, for example, to lend information or to archive it."[9] Digital Rights Management (DRM) involves the ability of copyright holders to dictate how digital content is used and the technologies that may monitor such use. "While copyright holders have exclusive rights of copyright—such as the right to make a copy or the right to distribute a work to the public—thus far they have not had the right to control how works can be used (the right to see a work, for example, or to read a work)."[10]

The official stance of the Association of Research Libraries concerning fair use is encapsulated in a working document titled *Fair Use in the Digital Age.* It defines the lawful uses of copyrighted works by individuals, libraries, and educational institutions in the electronic environment.[11]

As it is written now, this position statement declares that the public has a right to access. This right should include the ability to browse, read, listen to, or view materials in whatever format they may be available. It states:

Without infringing copyright, the public has a right to expect

- to read, listen to, or view publicly marketed copyrighted material privately, on site or remotely;
- to browse through publicly marketed copyrighted material;
- to experiment with variations of copyrighted material for fair use purposes, while preserving the integrity of the original;
- to make or have made for them a first generation copy for personal use of an article or other small part of a publicly marketed copyrighted work or a work in a library's collection for such purpose as study, scholarship, or research; and
- to make transitory copies if ephemeral or incidental to a lawful use and if retained only temporarily.

Without infringing copyright, nonprofit libraries and other Section 108 libraries, on behalf of their clientele, should be able

- to use electronic technologies to preserve copyrighted materials in their collections;
- to provide copyrighted materials as part of electronic reserve room service;
- to provide copyrighted materials as part of electronic interlibrary loan service; and
- to avoid liability, after posting appropriate copyright notices, for the unsupervised actions of their users.

Users, libraries, and educational institutions have a right to expect

- that the terms of licenses will not restrict fair use or other lawful library or educational uses;
- that U.S. government works and other public domain materials will be readily available without restrictions and at a government price not exceeding the marginal cost of dissemination; and
- that rights of use for nonprofit education apply in face-to-face teaching and in transmittal or broadcast to remote locations where educational institutions of the future must increasingly reach their students.

Carefully constructed copyright guidelines and practices have emerged for the print environment to ensure that there is a balance between the rights of users and those of authors, publishers, and copyright owners.[12]

RECENT LEGISLATION

Digital Millennium Copyright Act

The Digital Millennium Copyright Act (DMCA) of 1998 resulted from the perceived need of publishing houses and information providers to develop electronic measures "which would allow copyright owners to enforce restrictions on use through sophisticated technological means."[13] Specifically, Section 1201 of the DMCA states,

"No person shall circumvent a technological measure that effectively controls access to a work protected under this title."[14] This prohibition on circumvention became effective on October 28, 2000. Furthermore, in Section 108 the DMCA specifically targets libraries by stating,

> The library must include the notice that appears on the work. This can be done by reproducing the page that contains this notice or by creating a rubber stamp with ©___ (for copyright owner). ___ (for year published) and filling in the notice information.[15]

Information stored electronically is much easier to reproduce, transmit to other users, reformat, and download from servers than print and analog materials. This has led to a major shift in the way businesses and policymakers think about intellectual property. It was much harder fifteen years ago to transmit a book or even an article from one place to another. It had to be mailed intact or photocopied, which was labor-intensive and expensive enough to discourage the average user. Electronic books, online databases, and Adobe Acrobat Reader have made dramatic changes in how people use libraries and in their expectations for accessibility.

Technology, Education, and Copyright Harmonization Act (TEACH Act)

Enacted October 3, 2002, by Congress, the TEACH Act is a complete revision of Section 110(2) of the U.S. Copyright Act. It strives to "strike a balance between protecting copyrighted works, while permitting educators to use those materials in distance education."[16] Its focus is on distance education, which has grown exponentially at many colleges and universities, as well as at primary and secondary institutions. The law is built on the premise that "distance education should occur in discrete installments, each within a confined space of time, and with all the elements integrated into a cohesive lecture-like package."[17]

To summarize, the TEACH Act does not give an institution carte blanche to reformat all of its videotapes for use in distance-learning classes. It does demand that an institution limit access to copyrighted works through the use of technological measures by students who are currently enrolled in the class and to limit their access to the time period needed to complete the class session. Not only does the TEACH Act require that access be limited, but it also requires that the institution implement, to the best that it can based on the limitations of technology, a means to prevent further copying and distribution of the copyrighted work. This is a tall order when something is digital; although the technology is starting to be available to do this, it is costly and puts the responsibility for enforcing copyright on the institution. Some institutions may decide that the TEACH Act may "impose an unreasonable burden on instructors or students. . . . After conducting this assessment, some institutions may choose to rely on other copyright exemptions rather than TEACH."[18]

A common theme for this and several other pieces of legislation still under discussion is that the interests of the copyright owner are beginning to take precedence over those of the patron. Restrictions and limitations abound, and the end is not yet in sight. Yet, with all of this legislation, the library still has options, the first and foremost being to exercise the right to negotiate a contract that contains language favorable toward fair use and to require a vendor to meet all applicable state regulations and laws. "Contracts to acquire materials for patrons' use that restrict the library's rights under Section 108 only affect the particular materials covered by the contract."[19] If a library assumes that the licensing agreement is a fair and equitable document without a thorough understanding of its content, then the library may waive valuable rights as they pertain to access and ownership. This can have a detrimental affect on the library's functioning and on its original mission.

Licensing agreements are a routine part of most libraries' business; they are a "legal means of controlling the use of their products [and] libraries need to be aware that licensing arrangements may restrict their legal rights and that of their users."[20] Before library personnel begin to negotiate any contract, it is advisable for them to have a good working relationship with the institution's copyright officer and the IT department and to have access to several key documents (which may or may not be readily available): guidelines for vendors that state what provisions the library expects to see contained in the contract, a model license that is customized for the library, and a set of policies and procedures for acquiring digital content. The negotiators should also have the ability to decide what other options are available if the vendor is unwilling or unable to address the library's concerns. If the institution needs to develop these documents or perhaps revise them, excellent resources are available online for ideas and guidance.[21,22]

IN-HOUSE USE

It should be apparent to the reader that when making purchasing decisions for electronic resources, many minefields are waiting for the unwary. If the library is open to the public yet the licensing agreement specifically states that only registered users of the institution may access materials held within that collection, then the library must have a way to restrict access. Some libraries find that the simplest solution is to require that all users, even those within the library, be asked to authenticate with a username and password. On the other hand, if the library has negotiated IP recognition for unlimited access within the confines of the library, but requires all off-site users to authenticate on campus and then be redirected to the resource as part of the licensing agreement, then requiring a password may be necessary only for patrons who are not physically present. A third variation is that the license is valid only for patrons who come in to the library, limiting access to online subscriptions, so that patrons who are off site are not included in the agreement. A close working relationship with the IT personnel will make the technical details much easier to understand. They can provide guidance and assistance to implement an authentication system and to troubleshoot any problems that arise from cookies and software products such as WebCT or AOL.

The following situation could occur and illustrates the need for a well-negotiated licensing agreement: an item was available within a database on a certain date when a faculty member was preparing for class. Before the class started, however, publication was sold to another publisher and the item disappeared from the database. If the faculty member made a hard copy of the item, is it fair use to place it on electronic reserve, or does this violate copyright? If you were to ask a copyright lawyer, the attorney would probably suggest that you consult your license agreement. Is this an area that your agreement covers? Would you want it to be covered?

OFF-SITE USE

Libraries were early adopters of the technology and infrastructure necessary to become institutions without physical limitations; when libraries began making resources and services available over the Internet, no one predicted that the future might include a tangle of laws and liabilities. The question that looms in the not-too distant future is whether libraries can negotiate licensing agreements and contracts that will continue to allow access to all patrons, not just the ones who can walk in the door. Distance learning has grown exponentially in the past ten years, with 16,539,000 undergraduate students enrolled during the 1999-2000 year.[23] Of that number, 59 percent were enrolled in Internet-based classes. The presence of the distance-learning student is changing forever the way libraries conduct their business; the demand for full-text resources is insatiable, and the more the library provides, the more the students want. This is illustrated by the student who e-mailed the reference desk and asked why the books listed in the library's catalog could not be accessed online. The library has almost 40,000 electronic books accessible as full text online through the catalog, and the student had assumed that all the items would be full text.[24]

When reference librarians deliver an article from a subscription database, are they circumventing the technological measure that controls access as mandated by the DMCA? The culture of the reference department is to assist the patron in locating and obtaining access to the information needed in the least restrictive manner possible. For example, when reference librarians receive e-mails from patrons who cannot access the databases at work because of a firewall and do not have Internet access at home, the librarians will often complete the search for the patrons and e-mail them a few selected articles. By doing so, however, the reference librarians may conceivably be breaching the DMCA. "In the terminology of the copyright law, a database is a 'compilation.' The Copyright Act defines a compilation as 'a work formed by the collection and assembling of preexisting materials or of data.' "[25] When patrons call the library and say that they do not own a computer or that their computer is not functioning properly, does the library have the right or obligation to fax them a printed copy? Obtaining provisions within a license agreement for these kinds of contingencies will result in better service for the user and better relations with the vendor. This means reading the fine print and perhaps consulting a lawyer who can assist with spotting potential problems. It also means having an acquisition policy in place that mandates certain criteria for all digital licensing contracts.

INTERLIBRARY LOAN
AND DOCUMENT DELIVERY

Interlibrary loan helps the library make sound financial decisions by allowing access to materials that may not be high-use items but that are still needed on occasion. "When an article is not available from an in-house collection or in full text from a database producer or online system, organizations may turn to document delivery or inter-library loan services."[26] No library can own every item ever printed, and they cannot possibly have access to every full-text resource available online. Resources sharing has become commonplace. "The information society has arrived, and with it, the digital student."[27] User demands can sometimes outstrip the library's ability to provide the article with little or no fee. What should the library do when a faculty member requests ten recent articles over a six-month period from the same journal? Should the library consider purchasing the item to support the faculty member's research needs? What prohibits the library from simply ordering the ten articles?

The National Commission on New Technological Uses of Copyrighted Works (CONTU) drafted a series of guidelines "to assist librarians and other copyright proprietors in understanding the amount of photocopying for use in interlibrary loan arrangements permitted under the copyright law."[28] However, as more periodicals become available in aggregated electronic collections and as prices continue to increase for print subscriptions, "publishers appear to be quite nervous that libraries are, in fact, competing with commercial service providers who pay royalties on each and every copy made and do not enjoy the benefit of the 'suggestion of five.' "[29] The suggestion of five is a guideline developed by CONTU and adhered to by libraries. It states,

> This guideline covers with respect to any given periodical (as opposed to any given issue of a periodical), filled requests of a library or archives (a "requesting entity") within any calendar

year for a total of six or more copies of an article or articles published in such periodical within five years prior to the date of the
request. These guidelines specifically shall not apply . . . to . . . an
article or articles published in any issue of a periodical, the publication date of which is more than five years prior to the date when
the request is made. These guidelines do not define the meaning,
with respect to such a request, of ". . . such aggregate quantities
as to substitute for a subscription to [such periodical]."[30]

What if a faculty member wishes to have articles from a journal
delivered to her office and the library does not own the print version,
but it does subscribe to a database that carries the journal but that limits
it to in-house use? Does this fall under fair use or under the DMCA?
Checking the licensing agreement would be one way of determining if
there are specific prohibitions against document delivery. What if another library requests an article from this database? When another library's request is for an item owned by the library, it is the responsibility of the interlibrary loan department to ask if the requesting
institution has complied with the CONTU guidelines. If the item is not
owned within the print collection, who determines if the item can be
loaned? Does the circulation department decide? Do the interlibrary
loan and acquisitions departments hammer out these kinds of questions
based on the licensing agreements and the institution's interpretation?

E-RESERVES

Electronic reserves (e-reserves) to support the curriculum are
becoming a standard color in the library palette. E-reserves open opportunities for faculty to provide standard reading materials to off-
campus students in the same way print reserves have for on-campus
students. E-reserves can provide access to photographs, slides, articles,
and even movie clips with just a few clicks of the mouse. Access can
be limited to a specific class by requiring an open-source software
program such as open source course reserve (OSCR) or by utilizing
the online public access catalog (OPAC) system coupled with a user-
authentication program such EzProxy. Properly managed, an online
course reserves system can be a real boon to on- and off-campus faculty and students.

Yet e-reserves have also become another piece of an increasingly complex puzzle, tangled within the framework of the TEACH Act, copyright law, and the DMCA. While the publishers of digital information are pushing for more legislation to better protect their interests, libraries are trying to resolve the technical and legal issues to provide reading and viewing materials online. The library wants to provide access and foster a relationship with its distant students and faculty but still comply with the copyright law.

When designing an e-reserve system, the library, and particularly its acquisitions personnel need to understand the limitations imposed by the licensing agreements of each vendor if an article from an online database is going to be used. Will it be a violation of the DMCA if the article is downloaded, perhaps reformatted as a pdf file, and uploaded to a password-protected area of the library's Web server or to a distance-learning server? What if a link was embedded within an online courseware package such as WebCT, and it contained an automatic password? Only with examination of the licensing agreement and discussion of fair use and the TEACH Act by all parties involved can a solid decision be reached.

Another wrinkle in the equation is copyrighted items that are now in the public domain. Database providers that have electronic versions of these items are pushing for copyright-like rights to them. For example, a journal such as *Sociometry,* which has been published since 1937 and has issues now in the public domain, has been indexed and scanned by a vendor that has an agreement with its publisher. The publisher, when contacted, states that the article in question is in the realm of the public domain, but the vendor's view is that its "sweat equity" gives it the rights to that article. How does the library obtain access to such an article? Should the library place the article on e-reserve after obtaining a print version from another library? Should the library be required to pay a fee to the vendor for the article? What if the article was not downloaded from the vendor's database? If HR 3261 passes, which would grant sweat equity rights to the vendor, which viewpoint (if it ever went that far) would win in court? My procedure would be to put the article on e-reserve after getting a written statement from the publisher that the item is in the public domain.

Consider the following situation. A faculty member approaches the library about a set of slides that are used in face-to-face classes. The teacher now wants to place the slides on e-reserve for use in distance-education classes. What would your library do? Because the materials would be used to enrich the learning experience and would be an integral part of the class experience, the request appears to be reasonable. Would one option be to scan and reformat the slides as jpg files? Would this reformatting be in compliance with the TEACH Act? Would it be wise to contact the vendor to determine if a digital set of the slides is now available? What if an instructor wanted to include clips from a movie such as *Hamlet*? The newer version is available on DVD, and clips could be chosen, but how would further copying be prevented? If the library used streaming video and audio, the user would need a high-speed Internet connection and a fairly new computer, but it would (with the state of current technology) prevent downloading and copying. If the library decided to use QuickTime, then the file could potentially be downloaded and redistributed, but the user would not necessarily need the fastest connection.

What if the instructor wanted to show the entire movie, as he or she might do if the class were meeting on campus? If the library owned an analog copy of the video, is the library's e-reserves the appropriate location for this file, or should the instructor be making arrangements with the campus IT department? If the movie is placed on the IT department's server, which may not have a means of authenticating students, is it covered by the TEACH Act? Granting a request for e-reserves is not as simple as saying yes. Format, technology, and the TEACH Act need to be considered. "In order to facilitate digital transmissions, the law permits digitization of some analog works, but only if the work is not already available in digital form."[31]

DISCUSSION

When purchasing decisions for print and online resources are made at you library, is one person in charge of the negotiating process, or is it a team effort? Does your institution work cooperatively with the campus IT department to determine best practices for access to online information sources? The best use will be made of online resources when library and IT personnel work together.

Institutions need guidelines for vendors that must be met in the licensing agreement. By including the IT department and other stakeholders, the library can develop policies and procedures that work with, not against, other licensing agreements that exist throughout the university. Although we all are averse to adding more committee meetings to already overcommitted schedules, this might be one way to create stronger working relationships with key partners. It could also foster a better understanding as to what each department actually does. After all, librarians know that they do not merely read books and look at magazines all day, and IT people know they do not run around with a coffee cup in their hands all day.

Harvard University library's Web site, http://hul.harvard.edu/ldi/resources/vendor_guidelines.pdf, contains a good example of vendor guidelines. The document clearly outlines the university's expectations for the vendor on a wide variety of issues, including definitions of users; authorized uses of materials (including interlibrary loans, and reserves); perpetual use rights; patron confidentiality; performance warranties; statistics; and contract precedence. If libraries implemented guidelines for vendors, much of the ambiguity concerning copyright could be removed. However, some level of ambiguity in the contract language will be necessary in order to cover unanticipated changes in technology and user needs. Other resources mentioned on the Harvard Web site about best practices for the acquisition of electronic information include the following:

- Principles for Licensing Electronic Resources (American Association of Law Libraries, et al.) accessible at http://www.arl.org/scomm/licensing/principles.html
- NERL Licensing Guidelines (NorthEast Research Libraries Consortium), accessible at http://www.library.yale.edu/NERLpublic/licensingprinciples.html

Does your library keep usage statistics to track what the patrons are requesting and using in person and online? Most database providers can supply lists of the most frequently and the least frequently accessed titles. This information, in conjunction with knowledge about overlap of titles across vendors and what print subscriptions, the library carries, provides a sound basis for making aquisition decisions. The costs of print and electronic journals and database subscriptions will continue to escalate. Libraries need ways to provide the highest quality information to scholars within the confines of their budget. For most libraries this means making some difficult and often unpopular choices. If the library has data with which to open dialog with faculty and board members to educate them on the financial realities of subscriptions, they will be more likely to make cost-effective and efficient decisions.

CONCLUSION

One of the major reasons why libraries were founded in America was to provide access to information for those who could not afford to purchase books, which were extremely expensive. With the advent of new technologies and new delivery methods, access to information has continued to be placed out of the financial reach of many individuals, yet access to information through the library portal can be done more seamlessly if the library has purchased the right to do so. The rise of information licensing, rather than purchasing, has provided increased opportunities for the reproduction rights organization and posed a threat to the convention of fair use. Copyright, fair use, and licensing agreements are not black and white issues. There are many shadings and nuances, which can muddy the issues of ownership, access, and law. Today, before copyrights are reassigned to the information brokers, libraries must defend a basic tenet: information should not be limited to those who can afford to pay for it. If libraries do not jump into the picture and make their voices heard, access to information, even much of that which is currently within the public domain, will be limited to those who can afford to pay for it. The future of the academic library is not gray; it is limited only by the number of colors we choose to place on our palette.

NOTES

1. These lists are taken from the Association of Research Libraries. *ARL Supplementary Statistics: Investments in Electronic Resources.* Chicago, IL. Cited November 18, 2003. Available online: http://www.arl.org/stats/sup/index.html.

2. George Pike. "The Delicate Dance of Database Licenses." *Computers in Libraries.* May 2002, pp. 12-14, 63-64.

3. Committee on Energy and Commerce. "House Rpt.108-437: Consumer Access to Information Act of 2004," March 2004, p. 2.

4. Ibid.

5. Committee on Energy and Commerce. "Bill Summary and Status for the 108th Congress," March 2004. Available online: http://thomas.loc.gov/cgi-bin/bdquery/z?d108:HR03261:@@@L&summ2=m&.

6. www.copyright.gov/title17/92chap1.htm#107.

7. Bernadette Murphy. "Washington Hotline: Copyright and Database." *College and Research Library News.* April 2004, p. 222.

8. Amy Metcalfe, Veronica Diaz, and Richard Wagoner. "Academe, Technology, Society, and the Market: Four Frames of Reference for Copyright and Fair Use." *Portal: Libraries and the Academy.* April 2003, 3(2): 191.

9. Doug Brown. "Libraries: Checking Out in the Digital Age." *Inter@ctive Week.* June 26, 2000, 7(25): 112, 5p, 5c.

10. ALA. *Digital Rights Management and Libraries.* Chicago: American Library Association. Cited November 20, 2003. Available online: http://www.ala.org/ala/washoff/WOissues/copyrightb/digitalrights/digitalrightsmanagement.htm.

11. *Fair Use in the Digital Age.* Chicago, IL: Association of Research Libraries. Cited October 10, 2003. Available online: http://www.arl.org/info/frn/copy/fairuse.html.

12. Ibid.

13. Ivy Anderson. *Harvard University Library Digital Initiative: Digital Acquisitions.* Cambridge, MA: Harvard University. Cited November 25, 2003. Available online: http://hul.harvard.edu/ldi/html/acquisitions.html.

14. Rulemaking on Exemptions from Prohibition on Circumvention of Technological Measures That Control Access to Copyrighted Works. Available online: http://www.copyright.gov/1201/anticirc.html.

15. Steven J. Melamut, Patricia L. Thibodeau, and Eric Albright. "Fair Use or Not Fair Use: That Is the Electronic Reserves Question." *Journal of Interlibrary Loan, Document Delivery & Information Supply,* 2000, 11(1): 3-29.

16. Kenneth D. Crews. *New Copyright Law for Distance Education: The Meaning and Importance of the TEACH Act.* Indianapolis, IN: Indiana University–Purdue University Indianapolis. Cited November 25, 2003. Available online: http://www.copyright.iupui.edu.

17. *Technology, Education and Copyright Harmonization Act, U.S. Code* 17 (2002), §101.

18. *Technological Requirements of the TEACH Act.* Chicago, IL: American Library Association. Cited October 23, 2003. Available online: http://www.ala.org/washoff/WOissues/copyrightb/distanceed/teachdrm.pdf.

19. Stephanie C. Ardito, Paula Eiblum, and Renee Daulong. "Realistic Approaches to Enigmatic Copyright Issues Online." *Wilton.* May/June 1999, 23(3): 91-95.

20. Mary M. Case, "Library Associations Endorse Principles for Licensing Electronic Resources." Available online: http://www.ala.org/ala/washoff/WOissues/copyrightb/distanceed/teachdrm.pdf.

21. *Principles for Licensing Electronic Resources* (American Association of Law Libraries, et al.). Chicago, IL. Cited November 25, 2003. Available online: http://www.arl.org/scomm/licensing/principles.html.

22. NERL Licensing Guidelines (NorthEast Research Libraries Consortium) [online]. New Haven, CT: Cited November 25, 2003. Available online: http://www.library.yale.edu/NERLpublic/licensingprinciples.html.

23. U.S. Census Bureau. *United States Statistical Abstract.* No. 267: Undergraduates in Post Secondary Institutions Taking Distance Education Courses: 1999-2000. Washington, DC.

24. Cannon Memorial Library. Ask a Librarian. Question asked November 29, 2003.

25. University of Texas System, Office of the General Counsel. *Copyright Crash Course: Copyright in the Library; Interlibrary Loan.* Austin: University of Texas System. Cited November 19, 2003. Available online: http://www.utsystem.edu/ogc/IntellectualProperty/cprtindx.htm#top.

26. American Library Association. *Principles for Licensing Electronic Resources.* Chicago: ALA. Cited November 21, 2003. Available online: http://www.arl.org/scomm/licensing/principles.html.

27. Van Kampen. *Library Anxiety, the Information Search Process, and Doctoral Students' Use of the Library,* p. 2.

28. National Commission on New Technological Uses of Copyrighted Works. *Final Report of the National Commission on New Technological Uses of Copyrighted Works,* July 31, 1978, Library of Congress, Washington, DC, pp. 54-55.

29. University of Texas System, Office of the General Counsel. *Copyright Crash Course: Copyright in the Library; Interlibrary Loan.* Austin: University of Texas System. Cited November 26, 2003. Available online: http://www.utsystem.edu/ogc/IntellectualProperty/cprtindx.htm#top.

30. Coalition for Networked Information Policies. *A Compilation of Position Statements, Principles, Statutes, and Other Pertinent Statements.* Washington, DC. Cited November 26, 2003. Available online: http://www.cni.org/docs/infopols/CONTU.html.

31. Crews. *New Copyright Law for Distance Education: The Meaning and Importance of the TEACH Act.* Indianapolis: Indiana University–Purdue University. Available online: http://www.copyright.iupui.edu.

Chapter 2

Copyright and Fair Use: Electronic Reserves

Linda Neyer

INTRODUCTION

Any discussion of library electronic reserves programs must begin with the issue of copyright. Copyright law is, of course, extremely complex. Certain exceptions to the law, such as the fair use exception, were written into the law in purposefully vague language to allow for future developments.[1] In addition, recent legislation and court cases prompted by technological developments contribute to copyright law complexity. It is crucial that those in charge of an electronic reserves program have a good grasp of the basic copyright issues, to strike a balance between copyright infringement, resulting in possible litigation, and excessive caution, resulting in overcompliance and unnecessary expenditure of funds in times of shrinking budgets.

This chapter is intended as a basic primer on copyright issues for those establishing and operating an electronic reserves program, not only librarians but also administrators and information technology personnel. Individuals wanting more detailed, up-to-date information are urged to consult the Web sites listed throughout and at the end of the chapter.

The chapter first examines the past and present development of copyright law as it affects library reserves programs, especially electronic reserves programs, and focuses specifically on the fair use

The author wishes to thank Bonnie Strohl, associate director of the Weinberg Memorial Library, University of Scranton, for her invaluable help in the writing of this chapter.

doi:10.1300/5580_02

21

exception to copyright law. It next focuses on how the law affects the actual implementation of an electronic reserves program and offers practical suggestions for establishing policies and procedures.

BASIC COPYRIGHT LAW

Copyright is what its name implies: the right to make and distribute copies of an original work. Copyright can be thought of as marketing rights, the rights of copyright holders to sell their works and be free from the threat of pirated copies that diminish the market for their works.[2]

In essence, copyright creates a limited monopoly on the use of a copyrighted work, limited in the sense that a balance must be struck between the rights of the copyright holder and the rights of individuals to use the copyrighted work to advance their knowledge and learning.[3] The sole intention of the law is not to benefit copyright owners but primarily to benefit the public good. The purpose of the law is to "promote the progress of science and of the useful arts," not to ensure payment to authors and publishers.[4]

Copyright law in the United States is based upon the copyright clause of the U.S. Constitution, the current copyright statute, the Copyright Act of 1976, and the copyright decisions of the U.S. Supreme Court. The complete text of the copyright law may be found on the U.S. Copyright Office's Web site, http://www.copyright.gov/ title17/.

The Copyright Act of 1976, Title 17, U.S. Code, Sections 101-1332, defines key terms, establishes the categories of protected materials, the duration of a copyright holder's rights, exceptions to the regulations, amendments to Title 17, and related treaties and legislation. Recent additions to the law include the Sonny Bono Copyright Term Extension Act of 1998, which extended the previous term of copyright protection by twenty years. Although seen by many as protecting the interests of the entertainment industry, the act was nevertheless upheld by the Supreme Court in its January 2003 ruling on *Eldred v. Ashcroft*.[5]

Another addition to the law passed in 1998 was the Digital Millennium Copyright Act (DMCA), which attempted to update the law to protect digital works. However, in the view of many, the DMCA failed to strike a balance between the holders of copyrights and the users of copyrighted material, erring instead by giving preference to copyright holders.[6] The TEACH (Technology, Education, and Copyright Harmonization) Act of 2002 has to some extent rectified this imbalance and has been largely welcomed by the academic community as expanding educators' rights to use materials in distance learning.[7]

Other forms of intellectual property, including patents and trademarks, will not be discussed in detail. Patents and trademarks are registered with the U.S. Patent and Trademark Office, an agency of the U.S. Department of Commerce. It is important to distinguish among copyright, patents, and trademarks, as different rights and penalties for infringement are associated with each. The law on trademark protects logos, symbols, slogans, titles, and designs that uniquely identify a product from others in its field. Patent law protects processes, methods, systems, devices, and ideas. For a useful discussion of the differences among copyright, patents, and trademarks, consult the U.S. Patent and Trademark Office Web site, http://www.uspto.gov/web/offices/pac/doc/general/whatis.htm.

Copyright protects original works of creative expression, including the following:

1. Literary works such as books, articles, reports, and poems
2. Musical compositions and recordings
3. Dramatic works including accompanying music
4. Pictorial, graphic, and sculptural works such as photographs, paintings, drawings, and charts
5. Audiovisual materials such as films, videos, and animations
6. Performance pieces such as choreography, pantomimes, plays, and television programs
7. Architecture and blueprints
8. Computer programs, Web pages, Java applets, and video games
9. Works by an author for compilation and derivative works that result in an original work (Prior permission is required for works compiled, and protection extends only to the contribution of the author.)

This discussion focuses on literary works such as books, articles, reports, and poems—the types of work most frequently placed in electronic reserves systems.

A work is protected by copyright once the work is fixed in a tangible form, even if only one copy exists. It is not necessary to include the copyright notice, or the symbol ©, with the name of the owner of the copyright and the copyright date. Therefore, the absence of a copyright notice does not mean that a work is in the public domain, free for all to use. However, fixing the date and owner and registering the copyright with the Copyright Office is necessary to recover damages in court and to protect against pirated copies and infringement. The Copyright Office's Web site is http://www.copyright.gov/.

Copyright does not protect works published before 1923 because they have entered the public domain; facts; blank forms for collecting information; URLs and works such as telephone books that are not the product of an original author; and U.S. government publications. Works created after January 1, 1978, are protected for the life of the author plus seventy years. To make the term limits on copyright understandable, Laura Gasaway, at the University of North Carolina, has created a very helpful chart, "When Works Pass into the Public Domain," available at http://www.unc.edu/~unclng/public-d.htm. Anything in the public domain may be used freely without permission; however, a work does not pass into the public domain simply because it becomes out of print.

The rights of the copyright owner are exclusive. Only he or she may obtain profit from the work and control how his or her creative effort is used and presented. There are six exclusive rights:

1. To reproduce the original work in copies
2. To produce derivative works based on the copyrighted work (i.e., to modify the original)
3. To distribute copies of the work to the public by sale, transfer of ownership, rental, or lease
4. To perform the work publicly
5. To display the work publicly
6. To perform sound recordings by digital audio transmission

No one other than the copyright holder can exercise these rights, but the copyright holder may assign certain rights to others or give permission for another party to use the work. In the case of electronic reserves, under some circumstances libraries request permission to reproduce the original work in a digital copy.

Identifying who the copyright owner is can sometimes be problematic. The copyright owner in most cases is the original author(s).

In "works for hire"—those works created by employees as a part of their job—the employer owns the copyright. Works for hire also include those for which an independent contractor is specifically hired, and exceptions to these categories may be made by written agreements. In the case of periodicals, the publisher usually acquires all rights from the contributing authors before publication, often including the authors' right to distribute copies of their own works.

Duane Webster and others concerned with access to scholarly information have suggested that authors negotiate to retain some control over their intellectual property.[8] Some publishers do grant authors certain rights, including making copies for personal or classroom use and reusing any portion of the work in a future publication.[9] Jeff Rosedale has listed on his Web site the names of publishers with a history of giving permission for use of their material for electronic reserves: http://www.mville.edu/Administration/staff/Jeff_Rosedale/.

Penalties for copyright infringement can be quite harsh: the court may award statutory damages to the copyright holder at a minimum of $750 up to a maximum of $30,000 for each infringement (that is, each document or item that was used unlawfully). If the infringement is found to be willful, the fines can be increased up to $150,000 per infringement. However, if you work for a nonprofit educational institution, including a library, and can show that you were acting in good faith, not intending to infringe copyright but acting in the belief that your use was a fair one, the court can reduce the statutory award to $0 even if you are found guilty of copyright infringement.[10] In May, 2005, the university librarians at the University of California-San Diego (UCSD) issued a statement disputing assertions made by the Association of American Publishers (AAP) "that the electronic reserves at the UCSD library violate federal copyright law because the amount of posted material exceeds 'fair use'." As of December, 2005, the AAP had not yet filed suit against UCSD, perhaps because they began litigation against the Google Print for Libraries Project in October, 2005.[11]

THE DISCUSSION OF FAIR USE

To balance the rights of copyright holders against the public good, Congress wrote several exceptions into copyright law, including the fair use provision, Section 107 of Title 17, under which reserves programs have historically operated.[12]

The fair use provision allows the use of a work for purposes of "criticism, comment, news reporting, teaching (including multiple copies for classroom use), scholarship, or research" under certain criteria; however, there are no clear-cut rules for application of the criteria—and only the courts can determine authoritatively whether a use is fair. Each case requires an individual analysis, and no single factor determines, by itself, whether a use is fair; it is more a balance of factors.[13] That being said, the criteria that determine fair use are as follows:

1. *The purpose and character of use.* This criterion examines whether the use is for a commercial purpose (which tends to weigh against fair use) or for a nonprofit, educational purpose (which tends toward fair use). Because most educational institutions and libraries are nonprofit and noncommercial, their use of a work tends more toward fair use.
2. *The nature of the work.* Works of fact versus works of fiction lend themselves more readily toward fair use. The concern here is whether the use of the work is for entertainment or for scholarly purposes.[14]
3. *The amount and substantiality of portion copied.* Copying a limited part and not the "heart" of a work points more toward fair use (this is a qualitative as well as a quantitative measure).
4. *The effect on market value.* This criterion assesses what the effect on the market value of the work will be.

Depending on the analysis of the first three factors, the fourth factor may not be taken into consideration. The fourth factor asks if the use were widespread and were not a fair use, would the copyright owner lose money; it does not ask whether the copyright owner would lose money if the use were fair. It boils down to this:

Courts deal with this propensity of the fourth factor to encourage circular reasoning by looking at the first three factors before evaluating the fourth. If the first three factors indicate that the use is likely fair, courts will not permit the fourth factor to convert an otherwise fair use to an infringing one. On the other hand, if the first three factors indicate that the use is likely not fair, courts are willing to consider lost revenues under the fourth factor. . . . This means that if a use is tipping the balance in favor of fair use after the first three factors, the fourth factor should not affect the results, even if there is a market for permissions, even if the owner would lose money because of the use.[15]

On the other hand, although libraries can claim fair use for works placed in electronic reserves, there is still a market factor to be evaluated. The courts have taken new technology into consideration and are listening to publishers' arguments that they are losing licensing royalties. Higher education represents a market for textbook publishers, and if educators did not use services such as electronic reserves, many would opt to have students purchase textbooks or other reading materials to supplement the courses.[16] An argument can be made that the void in the textbook market should be made up through licensing fees or permission fees. By facilitating compliance, the Copyright Clearance Center (CCC) (http://www.copyright.com) has, in effect, created a market for permission fees. In the case of *American Geophysical Union v. Texaco,* the court found that the services offered by the CCC provided both additional revenue to the publisher and added value to the copyright at a "reasonable cost and burden" to the user.[17]

To help people deal with the ambiguity of fair use, Congress approved the Agreement on Guidelines for Classroom Copying in Not-for-Profit Educational Institutions with Respect to Books and Periodicals in 1976. The guidelines do not have the force of law but were intended to provide guidance for people uncertain about fair use in academic settings. The guidelines have limited application for electronic reserves; they do not mention libraries, and they were intended as a minimum, not a maximum. Therefore, it is possible that a use that exceeds the numbers in the guidelines will be considered a fair use.[18]

The guidelines stipulated the following criteria:

1. *Brevity*—This is defined as an article of 2,500 words or less or an excerpt of 1,000 words or 10 percent, whichever is less, but a minimum of 500 words.
2. *Spontaneity*—The use must be at the direction of the individual teacher and not at that of the institution; the use must not be intended to substitute for a text but for late-breaking, current information that a teacher wants to include at the last minute.[19]

3. *Cumulative effects*—The work can be used for only one course (even if there are multiple sections); it may not be used from term to term; only one article or other work from an author or two excerpts from an author, and no more than three from a periodical volume or other collective work, can be copied and distributed.

In addition, the guidelines required that each copy include a notice of copyright and that the student not be charged for articles beyond the cost of copying.

In 1982, the American Library Association adopted its ALA Model Policy, which essentially restated the Classroom Guidelines with specific reference to the use of reserves in libraries. Many academic libraries followed this policy or another one closely modeled on it despite the fact that the policy was not been endorsed by any organization other than ALA.[20] Among several provisions, the policy states in essence that reserves should not replace textbooks but complement them; that the same material cannot be used from one semester to another; that a copyright notice should be listed on the first page; and that the market should not be affected—that is, the library should own at least one copy.[21] Interestingly, the policy is no longer available on the ALA's Web site.

In 1994, a Conference on Fair Use (CONFU) was convened as part of President Clinton's Information Infrastructure Task Force with the purpose of bringing together copyright owners (i.e., publishers) and users of copyrighted works (i.e., librarians and academicians) to come to an agreement on how these works may be displayed digitally.[22]

By 1998, when CONFU ended, no group had reached an agreement on a definition of fair use except for the educational multimedia group, which adopted a set of guidelines (see "Fair Use Guidelines for Educational Multimedia" on the University of Texas Web site at http://www.utsystem.edu/ogc/intellectualproperty/ccmcguid.htm). Most members of the library community, including representatives of ALA and the Association of Research Libraries (ARL), as well as university presses and the Association of American Publishers, would not adopt the final Electronic Reserves Guidelines, completed by a committee. The library community felt the definition was too restrictive, and the publishers felt it was not restrictive enough.[23]

Although never approved, the guidelines are still followed by some libraries, in particular, the requirements that an article or chapter can be used for only one semester, that access to materials must be restricted to students enrolled in the course, that material contain a warning that further transmission of the material is prohibited by law, and that bibliographic access to reserve material be limited to the course name, course number, and the name of the instructor.

The latest development in the discussion of electronic reserves within the library community has been the circulation of ARL's recent statement "Applying Fair Use in the Development of Electronic Reserves," written by Georgia Harper, manager of the Intellectual Property Section of the University of Texas System Office of General Counsel, and Peggy Hoon, scholarly communication librarian at North Carolina State University, available at http://www.arl.org/access/eres/eresfinalstmt.shtml. The statement has been endorsed by the Association of College and Research Libraries, the American Library Association, the Association of Law Libraries, the Medical Library Association, and the Special Libraries Association, and it was drafted as a response to confusion about the passage of the TEACH Act of 2002. The document stresses the importance of relying on the four fair use factors as the basis for an electronic reserves policy.

Harper and Hoon note,

> There is no fair use checklist, and there is no need to import from other sections of the law the detailed checklists of conditions, prohibitions, and exclusions that characterize their approach. . . . While there is no guarantee that a practice or combination of practices is fair use, such certainty is not required to safely implement e-reserves. The law builds in tolerance for risk-taking. . . . Each institution's combination of practices reflects its tolerance for risk against the background of prevailing beliefs about fair use. Understandably, "not knowing" makes many people uncomfortable, so Congress explicitly addressed this aspect of fair use. Section 504(c)(2) of the Copyright Act provides special protection to nonprofit libraries, educational institutions and their employees. When we act in good faith, reasonably believing that our actions are fair use, in the unlikely event we are actually sued over a use, we will not have to pay statutory damages even if a court finds that we were wrong. This demonstrates Congressional acknowledgement of the importance of fair use and *the importance of our using it!*[24]

A number of libraries have adopted the fair use provisions of Section 107 of the Copyright Act as the primary basis for their electronic reserves policies and are listed on ARL's Web site, http://www.arl. org/access/eres/erespolicies.shtml. A number of libraries are also using language to the effect that electronic scanning and posting of print, copyright-protected materials is an area of "unsettled law" and that they will be monitoring legal developments concerning fair use.

APPLYING COPYRIGHT LAW
TO ELECTRONIC RESERVES

When implementing an electronic reserves program, administrators will first need to clarify their institution's stance on how the fair use of copyrighted material will be defined. All material to be put on electronic reserves should be assumed to be copyright-protected unless it is clearly in the public domain. For copyrighted materials, electronic reserves administrators will need to determine whether the material may be used without obtaining permission (under the fair use exception to copyright law) or whether permission from the copyright holder must be obtained.

The development of policies and procedures for electronic reserves will be affected by various institutional variables. These variables include the institution's overall risk tolerance for litigation, the institutional culture with regard to the level of service that faculty expect from the library, and, of course, fiscal considerations.

The Institution's Overall Risk Tolerance for Litigation

Administrators of electronic reserves programs will want to consult with their institutions' counsel in order to define what will and will not be considered fair use of copyrighted materials. The University of Colorado Library identified four possible scenarios with regard to risk that are applicable to all academic libraries.[25]

1. *Limited service*—Only materials with no copyright issues may be placed on electronic reserves, including links to electronic journal articles to which the library subscribes.
2. *Full service with a broad interpretation of fair use*—Fair use will be claimed for all items owned by the library. For items not

owned by the library, royalties will be paid to the CCC or to the publisher directly for using copyrighted books and journal articles. If the library is unable to obtain permission for an item, then it will not be placed on electronic reserves.

3. *Full service with a narrow interpretation of fair use*—Only the first time use of an item will be considered "fair use"; subsequent uses will require obtaining permission.

4. *Full service with no fair use claimed*—All items must be cleared with the CCC or the publisher.

It seems likely that many libraries will, at least initially, follow the third scenario—full service with a narrow interpretation of fair use—based on the policies posted on many academic library Web sites.

The Institutional Culture with Regard to the Level of Service Faculty Expect from the Library

Basically, this factor addresses whether faculty will manage the work of putting their items on reserves, including locating the original document, scanning, and obtaining copyright clearance, or whether the library will manage it. In a 1999 survey, ARL reported that the ratio of libraries to faculty handling copyright issues was about 1:1.[26]

The obvious advantage to having libraries manage copyright permissions is that librarians have experience dealing with publishers and can more efficiently perform the necessary tasks. If the library handles copyright issues for electronic reserves, then the policies must be clearly defined and worded to give faculty realistic expectations.

Policies should be stated on request forms or Web pages and may include the following:

1. The institutional rules for copyright, clearly articulated.
2. The specific information faculty should provide to the library to be in compliance with copyright law:
   a. the number of students in the course
   b. the dates of the course (beginning and end)
   c. the number of sections
   d. the course number
   e. the name of the instructor
   f. full bibliographic information for the item

3. A reminder that if permission cannot be obtained to place an item on electronic reserves, then faculty have the option to place it on traditional reserves. Items that cannot be digitized and placed on electronic reserves would include an entire book, or almost an entire book, or more than two articles from the same journal. Likewise, standardized tests, entire course-packs, or "consumable" resources such as workbooks cannot be digitized and put on electronic reserves without copyright clearance as they do not meet the criteria for fair use.[27]

4. An explanation that passwords are used to access course electronic reserves and are given only to students enrolled in the course. Materials will be removed at the completion of the course.

5. A statement that a notice of copyright will be posted with each article, including the original copyright notice if available (e.g., Copyright © 2004 by Jane Doe) as well as a warning that further distribution is in violation of copyright law.

6. A statement that if a professor's own journal articles are to be put on reserve, then the library needs evidence that he or she has retained the right to do so in order to avoid copyright infringement.

7. A statement that the library needs to obtain written permission from any student whose materials are to be put on reserve under the Family Educational Rights and Privacy Act (FERPA).[28]

8. A note to the effect that electronic reserves may include core materials, not just "supplemental" readings.[29]

9. Information about the length of processing time for items that meet the criteria for fair use (this will obviously depend on the work flow) as well as for those items that do not meet fair use criteria (as long as six to eight weeks to obtain permission). If the library chooses to put up their electronic reserves as pending, as many do, then it also needs to include a note to the effect that if permission is denied then the item will have to be taken down.

10. A reminder that faculty also have access to a wide range of electronic journals for which the library has already paid and that they are encouraged and supported by the library to explore and use these journals for electronic reserves.

Fiscal Considerations

This issue concerns the bottom line of who will pay royalties to copyright holders—the library, individual academic departments, or another institutional unit. If the library pays, then decisions about limits will likely need to be made. Will the library establish a limit per department, per class, or per professor? Some institutions have chosen to set a limit of twenty articles, for example, that may be placed on electronic reserves for a single course.[30]

OBTAINING PERMISSION

Once it has been determined that permission from the copyright holder is necessary, the library may opt to use the CCC, or it may opt to contact copyright holders directly for permissions.[31]

The Copyright Clearance Center

Established in 1978 to facilitate compliance with the Copyright Act of 1976, the CCC states on its Web site, http://www.copyright. com, that it "currently manages rights relating to over 1.75 million works and represents more than 9,600 publishers and hundreds of thousands of authors and other creators."

The advantage of using the CCC is speed: if a copyrighted work is preauthorized with the CCC, permission may be granted almost immediately. In addition, the CCC offers a relatively cost-effective way of managing permissions. On March 15, 2004, the CCC began charging a standard flat fee of $3.00 for each granted license; there is no longer a processing fee for denied or cancelled permissions.[32]

In addition to this processing fee, the user may be charged a royalty by the copyright holder. There is no "standard" royalty: a publisher/copyright owner may charge no royalty, it may charge a nominal fee under $20, or it may charge in excess of $500. An exorbitant fee may serve the same purpose as denying permission.[33] Royalty fees may also vary depending on the date of publication, the number of pages to be used, and the number of students accessing the material. Some publishers registered with the CCC do allow users to get an "instant" royalty quote; however, many require that users contact them directly.[34]

The CCC does not advise clients whether they should obtain copyright permission to use a particular item; in other words, they will not determine for you if a use is "fair" or not. A quick perusal of their site might leave one with the impression that any use of copyrighted material requires permission, but this is, of course, not true. "Not all copying 'requires' that permission be obtained and royalties paid. Some copying without permission is permitted under both the fair use and library-use exemptions."[35] Because the CCC's role in developing a market for copyright holders has been cited in various court cases, it behooves individual libraries to avoid overcompliance to avoid establishing precedent.

Do-It-Yourself Permission Seeking

Some libraries prefer to contact publishers directly as a cost-saving measure rather than using the CCC; however, this approach is, of course, more time-consuming. Even those libraries that do use the CCC may need to resort to this approach to contact copyright holders who are not registered with the CCC. It is probably good practice to maintain a current database of information about publishers who have been previously contacted.

Information about publishers is readily available in the standard trade sources, *Ulrich's International Periodicals Directory* and *Books in Print,* or online via a Web search engine. The University of Texas Web site has extensive lists of links for contacting copyright holders (see "Getting Permission," http://www.utsystem.edu/ogc/intellectual property/permissn.htm).

There are many sites with sample letters requesting copyright permission, but generally a letter asking permission should include the following:

1. Complete bibliographic information about the item to be used, including number of pages
2. Detailed description of how the work will be reproduced and distributed
3. Complete information on the course for which the work is to be used, including number of students, number of sections, time taught, and so on

To expedite the permission-seeking process, it is acceptable to telephone publishers, who vary greatly in their practice. They may grant permission over the phone, they may request a formal letter, or they may grant permission via their Web site. If a publisher does give verbal permission, follow up the telephone conversation with a letter to have a written record.

Jeff Rosedale lists publishers on his Electronic Reserves Clearinghouse site who have a history of granting permissions for electronic reserves (http://www.mville.edu/Administration/staff/Jeff_Rosedale/) and notes that some publishers grant blanket permission to print subscribers.[36] Other publishers or copyright holders may charge royalties for each use. On occasion, permission to use a work may be denied, but generally stiff royalty fees have the same effect in discouraging use.[37] For this reason, libraries may want to set some limits on the amount of money they will pay either per article or per faculty member.

Some publishers or copyright holders may ask to view their work once it has been placed on electronic reserves, presumably to verify that sufficient "controls" are being used for access. Because it is best practice to permit access to only those students enrolled in the course via password, libraries may want to prepare an alternate password-protected page for publishers to view a single article.[38]

LINKING TO ELECTRONIC DATABASES

It seems self-evident to state that, whenever possible, libraries should link to articles in the electronic databases for which they are already paying licensing fees rather than digitizing print materials. Libraries spend millions of dollars for access to these databases, and one can legitimately ask why this is so if the sources are not being used.[39] Whenever possible, faculty should be encouraged and supported to use these resources. This is an area of outreach for librarians to work with faculty.

Librarians will want to consider several factors when dealing with vendors regarding electronic reserves. First, in order to link to a document in a database for electronic reserves, the library needs a stable URL for that document. The inability of a vendor to provide durable links may detract from that vendor's desirability. Also, when negotiating contracts with database vendors or reviewing an existing contract, find out if vendors place any limits on linking to items in a database.

For instance, some vendors limit the number of files that can be linked to at a given time; this may also be a practice that detracts from a vendor's desirability.

CONCLUSION

In the past, libraries relied on the fair use exception in copyright law to protect themselves from charges of copyright infringement when putting materials on library reserves. With the digitization of print sources, the situation has become more complex. Nevertheless, libraries have come full circle as they once again are relying on fair use to justify placing materials on electronic reserves. Readers are urged to consult the ARL-ERESERVE e-mail list (http://www.cni. org/Hforums/arl-ereserve/) for a continuing discussion of the topic. Of great importance is the discussion of repeated use. Some libraries appear to be claiming that if they subscribe to a journal, they may use any article from it for electronic reserves with no time restrictions and without obtaining permission. It seems likely that this issue of repeated use will be litigated at some point, and its resolution will obviously have great financial import for all academic libraries.

Meanwhile, electronic reserves may strengthen the role of the library in academia on several counts. By helping faculty navigate the morass of copyright law, librarians can perform a real service to their institutions, not only by helping them to avoid litigation but also by promoting the ethical use of information on campus, one of the objectives of information literacy.[40] Properly done, electronic reserves can strengthen the perception of librarians as "partners in instruction for the twenty-first century and as technology-savvy information providers on campus."[41] Furthermore, the issue of electronic reserves may prove to be an important factor in the scholarly communications discussion as it seeks to balance the rights of copyright holders with the rights of individuals to advance their knowledge and learning.

APPENDIX: RECOMMENDED WEB SITES

American Library Association. Copyright. http://www.ala.org/washoff/ WOissues/copyrightb/copyright.htm. ALA maintains a very current Website on copyright with the latest copyright news and legislation.

Association of Research Libraries Web Sites

- Applying Fair Use in the Development of Electronic Reserves Systems. http://www.arl.org/access/eres/eresfinalstmt.shtml. The recent statement written by Georgia Harper and Peggy Hoon asserting the right to fair use for electronic reserves can be accessed here.
- ARL-ERESERVE Forum. http://www.cni.org/Hforums/arl-ereserve/. An open list with browsable archives, the ARL-ERESERVE Forum is essential reading for anyone responsible for electronic reserves.
- Electronic Reserves Copyright Policies Based on Fair Use. http://www.arl.org/access/eres/erespolicies.shtml. This site provides links to libraries that have used the fair use provisions of Section 107 of the Copyright Act as the basis for their electronic reserves policies.

Copyright Clearance Center. Copyright Clearance Center: Permissions Made Easy. http://www.copyright.com. Areas to explore include the Academic Permissions Service (APS) Frequently Asked Questions and the Electronic Course Content Service (ECCS) Frequently Asked Questions.

Gasaway, Lolly. When U.S. Works Pass into the Public Domain. http://www.unc.edu/~unclng/public-d.htm. Lolly Gasaway of the University of North Carolina maintains this useful Web site, which gives the criteria for determining whether an item is in the public domain.

Indiana University-Purdue University, Indianapolis. Copyright Management Center. http://www.copyright.iupui.edu/index.htm. Look here for information pertaining to music and multimedia works. Kenneth Crews, a librarian, lawyer, and author of *Copyright Essentials for Librarians and Educators,* contributes to this site.

Rosedale, Jeff. Electronic Reserves Clearinghouse. http://www. mville. edu/Administration/staff/Jeff_Rosedale/. This is another extremely helpful site with many links to publishers and other libraries' policies. Jeff edited the book *Managing Electronic Reserves.*

Stanford University Libraries. Copyright and Fair Use. http://fairuse. stanford.edu/. This site is very helpful for its discussion of fair use, including numerous examples of court cases in which fair use was either upheld or rejected by the courts.

U.S. Copyright Office. Copyright Law of the United States. http:// www.copyright.gov/title17/. The full text of the copyright law and "all related laws contained in Title 17 of the United States Code" is on this Web site.

University of Texas. Crash Course in Copyright. http://www.utsystem. edu/ogc/IntellectualProperty/copypol2.htm. Probably the best place to start, this site has numerous pages on all aspects of copyright, including electronic reserves. Georgia Harper, who has written much of the information on this site, is the manager of the Intellectual Property Section of the University of Texas System, Office of General Counsel.

NOTES

1. Hoffman, Gretchen M. "Electronic Reserve Systems and Class-Based Web Pages." In *Copyright in Cyberspace: Questions and Answers for Librarians.* New York: Neal-Schuman, 2001, p. 132.
2. University of Georgia. *Regents Guide to Understanding Copyright and Educational Fair Use.* http://www.usg.edu/admin/legal/copyright/index.phtml. Accessed December 22, 2003.
3. Ibid.
4. Gasaway, Laura N. "Copyright Considerations for Electronic Reserves." In Jeff Rosedale (ed.), *Managing Electronic Reserves.* Chicago: American Library Association, 2002, p. 130.
5. Pike, George H. "Copyright and the CCC." *Information Today* 20(4), 2003: 17.
6. National Humanities Alliance. *Basic Principles for Managing Intellectual Property in the Digital Environment.* September 5, 2002. http://www.nhalliance. org/ip/ip_principles.html. Accessed May 13, 2003.
7. Bruwelheide, Janis H. "Re: Copyright Refresher CE?" In ARL-ERESERVE list [online discussion board]. November 6, 2002. https://mx2.arl.org/Lists/ARL-ERESERVE/Message/7026.html. Accessed November 11, 2003.
8. Webster, Duane. *The Practical Realities of the New Copyright Laws: A Librarian's Perspective.* Paper presented at the Modern Language Association Conference in New York City, December 28, 2002. http://www.arl.org/info/frn/copy/Webster MLA02.html. Accessed November 24, 2003.
9. *Academic Exchange Quarterly.* Manuscript Authentication & Copyright Agreement. http://www.rapidintellect.com/AEQweb/maca.htm. Accessed November 20,

2003. The publisher of *Academic Exchange Quarterly* states that the author "retains the right to reuse any portion of the work, without fee, in future works of the author's own" provided that the full citation and a notice of the journal's copyright are also included. Authors may make "digital or hard copies of part or all of this work for personal or classroom use without fee provided that copies are not made or distributed for profit or commercial advantage and that copies bear the full citation on the first page." The journal also permits free copyright clearance for any user other than the author, asking only that an online form be completed and submitted with a small processing fee.

10. Minow, Mary. "How I Learned to Love Fair Use . . . or How to Bring a $300,000 Lawsuit Down to $0 if You're a Library, Archive, or Nonprofit Educational Institution." Copyright and Fair Use: Stanford University Libraries. 2004. http://fairuse.stanford.edu/commentary_and_analysis/2003_07_minow.html. Accessed December 13, 2005.

11. "University Rejects American Association of Publisher's Claim that Electronic Reserves Violate Copyright Law." University of California, May 19, 2005. http://www.universityofcalifornia.edu/senate/news/source/UC.librarians.Msg.pdf. Accessed December 13, 2005; http://www.publishers.org/press/releases.cfm?PressReleaseArticleID=292.

12. Ibid., p. 114.

13. Ibid.

14. Hoffman, "Electronic Reserve Systems," p. 128.

15. University of Texas (UT). *Copyright Crash Course: Getting Permission.* http://www.utsystem.edu/ogc/intellectualproperty/permissn.htm. Accessed July 26, 2003. For other copyright permissions organizations, consult the University of Texas's Web site.

16. Metcalfe, Amy, Veronica Diaz, and Richard Wagoner. "Academe, Technology, Society, and the Market: Four Frames of Reference for Copyright and Fair Use." *Portal: Libraries and the Academy* 3(2) (2003): 191-206. In ProQuest [database online]. Cited November 25, 2003.

17. Pike, "Copyright and the CCC," p. 20.

18. Hoffman, "Electronic Reserve Systems," p. 131.

19. Gasaway, "Copyright Considerations," p. 117.

20. Ibid., p. 121.

21. Ibid., p. 120.

22. Van Draska, Meridee S. "Copyright in the Digital Classroom." *Journal of Allied Health* 32(3) (2003): 185-188. In ProQuest [database online]. Cited November 25, 2003.

23. Gasaway, "Copyright Considerations," p. 121.

24. Harper, Georgia and Peggy Hoon. *Applying Fair Use in the Development of Electronic Reserves Systems.* November 5, 2003. http://www.arl.org/access/eres/eresfinalstmt.shtml. Accessed November 11, 2003. Emphasis in original.

25. Austin, Brice and Karen Taylor. "Four Scenarios Concerning Fair Use and Copyright Costs: Electronic Reserves at the University of Colorado, Boulder." *Journal of Interlibrary Loan, Document Delivery & Information Supply* 13(3) (2003): 12. The University of Colorado Library, at the advice of its counsel, determined its risk tolerance supported adopting the second scenario for electronic reserves (full service with a broad interpretation of fair use).

26. Association of Research Libraries (ARL). *SPEC Kit 245: Electronic Reserves Operations in ARL Libraries.* 1999. http://www.arl.org/spec/245fly.html. Accessed November 26, 2003. An online flyer that summarizes the results of the print SPEC Kit.

27. UT, *Crash Course.*

28. Anderson, Judy and Lynne DeMont. "Treading Carefully Through the Murky Legalities of Electronic Reserves." *Computers in Libraries* 21(6) (2001): 42. In ProQuest [database online]. Accessed November 25, 2003.

29. Harper and Hoon, *Applying Fair Use.*

30. Rutgers University Libraries. *Reserve Services, A Guide for Faculty.* http://www.libraries.rutgers.edu/rul/lib_servs/reserve_services_faculty.shtml. Accessed January 12, 2004.

31. UT, *Crash Course.*

32. Copyright Clearance Center (CCC). Transactional Reporting Service. December 13, 2005. http://www.copyright.com/ccc/do/viewPage?pageCode=ac7-n> "BillingPolicy."

33. Ferullo, Donna L. "The Challenge of E-Reserves." *Library Journal Net Connect* (Summer 2002): 34. In ProQuest [database online]. Accessed November 25, 2003.

34. Schmidt, S. J. "Course Reserves, E-Reserves and Serving the Remote User." *Indiana Libraries* 19(1) (2000): 26. In WilsonWeb [database online]. Accessed May 15, 2003. Of 920 documents mounted on e-reserve at IUPUI in spring 1999, 365 required permission from copyright holders. Of these, less than 10 percent were denied (and were either never mounted or were immediately removed). Copyright holders granted permission for over 54 percent of requests; 36 percent failed to respond at all—these were accepted as permission granted by default. For that semester, IUPUI paid $6,850 in royalties for 197 documents to the CCC and other copyright holders.

35. Pike, "Copyright and the CCC," pp. 17, 20. The CCC has "evolved as both a passive factor and an active player" in the debate over fair use and library-use exemptions to the Copyright Act. In the case of *American Geophysical Union v. Texaco,* the court found that the services offered by the CCC provided both additional revenue to the publisher and added value to the copyright at a "reasonable cost and burden" to the user. In other words, the CCC has developed a market for copyright holders, although not necessarily intentionally.

36. Rosedale, Jeff. *Electronic Reserves Clearinghouse.* February 10, 2003. http://www.mville.edu/Administration/staff/Jeff_Rosedale/. Accessed May 3, 2003.

37. Ferullo, "The Challenge of E-Reserves," p. 34.

38. Association of Research Libraries (ARL). *ARL-ERESERVE Forum.* http://www.cni.org/Hforums/arl-ereserve/. Accessed November 10, 2003.

39. Ibid.

40. Association of College & Research Libraries (ACRL). *Information Literacy: Standard Five.* www.ala.org/ala/acrl/acrlstandards/informationliteracycompetency.htm.

41. Association of Research Libraries (ARL). *Transforming Libraries: Issue 1: Electronic Reserves.* http://www.arl.org/transform/eres/index.html. Accessed November 26, 2003.

Chapter 3

Evaluating Databases for Acquisitions and Collection Development

Audrey Powers

THE EVALUATION PROCESS

Faced with a plethora of databases, database trials, and database offers, librarians are beginning to realize that evaluating databases is a necessity. Evaluating existing database collections and determining which databases to add or remove from a library collection can become controversial and biased exercises, making purchase decisions a daunting task. To evaluate and compare databases in the most objective manner possible, initiation of a database evaluation program is appropriate. It guides librarians through the application of an assessment process in which final decisions about the disposition of a database, or group of databases, can be determined. It is the basis for a collaborative process with objective results.

The evaluation process is applicable when assessing one database or a collection of databases for acquisition, retention, and withdrawal purposes. Customizing the assessment process to an individual library's information needs is possible and encouraged. The assessment process includes identifying criteria, evaluating the databases, collating the data, reporting the data and results, and making final decisions regarding the disposition of each database. This process provides a means to guide informed, objective decision making. Initially developed for use with librarians, the process can be adapted for use with a variety of populations: students, faculty, librarians, and the public.

The following steps outline the development of a database evaluation program:

doi:10.1300/5580_03

- Phase I: Prepare
  —Determine criteria
  —Develop an evaluation form
  —Aggregate databases
  —Assign team leaders
  —Develop project timeline
- Phase II: Gather Data
  —Obtain known data
  —Distribute evaluation forms
  —Conduct evaluations
  —Collect completed evaluation forms
- Phase III: Results
  —Collate, analyze, and interpret data
  —Present data
  —Discuss results
  —Recommend an action plan

PHASE I

The first step is to determine which criteria are appropriate to include in the evaluation process. Base criteria selection decisions on the information needs of the library, the size and extent of the database collection, observed usage patterns, staffing levels, project timeline, and budget allocations. It is not always feasible to include all of the following criteria; therefore, select those integral to the objectives of the collection and the evaluation process.

Cost
Use
Cost per use
Duplication
Peer comparisons
Content
Unique content
Ease of use
Instruction
Overall quality
Need

Next, develop a database evaluation form that includes selected criteria important for the library to assess (see Exhibit 3.1). The Database Evaluation Form has two components: Known Data and Evaluations. Gather and collate known data before evaluating the databases. Known data include the following: cost (actual cost per year), use (usage statistics per year), cost per use (actual cost each time the database is used), duplication (duplication and comparison of full-text journal titles), and peer comparisons (databases available at peer institutions). Evaluations include these criteria: content, unique content, ease of use, instruction, overall quality, and need. Define and agree upon the definitions of each

EXHIBIT 3.1. Database Evaluation Form

Complete one form for each database

Database   _____
URL   _____
Evaluator   _____

Known Data

Cost:
Use:
Cost/use:
Duplication:
Peer comparisons:

Evaluations

Content: 0   1   2   3   4
Unique content: 0   1   2   3   4
Ease of use: 0   1   2   3   4
Instruction: 0   1   2   3   4
Overall quality: 0   1   2   3   4

     0 = Inappropriate 1 = Very Unsatisfactory 2 = Unsatisfactory
            3 = Satisfactory 4 = Very Satisfactory

Need: __ Inappropriate   __ Useful   __ Essential

Comments:

criterion before evaluating the databases, thus developing objective measures by which the evaluation process can occur. Answers to the following questions will assist with the formulation of a definition for each criterion:

1. Content
   What is the content of the database?
   Is the content appropriate for the intended audience?
   Is the reading level appropriate for the intended audience?
   Is the coverage selected or comprehensive?
   Is the content substantial?
   Are the journals scholarly journals?
   Is this the only database that covers this particular subject?
2. Unique content
   Are the journal titles unique to the database?
   Is the search interface common or unique?
   What are its special features?
3. Ease of use
   Is the format and layout easy to navigate?
   Is a standard search methodology in use?
   What retrieval methods are available (e-mail, print, and download options)?
   Is access to the database and search screen easy?
4. Instruction
   Is the database easy to teach?
   Is the number of simultaneous users limiting?
   Does the licensing agreement restrict class instruction?
   Is the database useful for assignments?
5. Overall quality
   Are there many errors?
   Is the database often inaccessible?
   Is the documentation adequate?
   Is the documentation useful, well written, and easy to navigate?
   Are use statistics available, in what format, and how often are they updated?
   Is technical assistance readily available?
6. Need
   What is the value to the library program?
   Is the database required?
   Does the database fulfill a need?

After the evaluation form is complete, compile a list of databases to evaluate and aggregate them by subject, discipline, type, or cost. Assign categorized groups of databases to team leaders who will accept responsibility to develop and honor the project timeline. They will be points of connection to the process as well as move the process forward. Their responsibilities include gathering the known data (cost, use, cost per use, duplication, and peer comparisons), distributing the evaluation forms, collecting the completed evaluation forms, collating the data, analyzing the results based on the given formula, presenting the data and results, and leading group discussions from which recommendations or final decisions are made. After the team leaders are in place, equitably distribute the databases and delineate the project timeline. Then the team leaders are ready to move the process forward.

PHASE II

During this part of the process, known data pertinent to the assessment process are gathered. Although this phase is labor-intensive, having the collated data available is useful when questions arise. For example, usage statistics and cost per use are viable measures of database activity. A standard, uniform presentation of usage statistics provided by database vendors is uncommon, inconsistent, and sometimes nonexistent. Two initiatives attempting to address this problem include ICOLC, International Coalition of Library Consortia, and COUNTER, Counting Online Usage of Networked Electronic Resources.

In *Guidelines for Statistical Measures of Usage of Web-Based Information Resources,* ICOLC established a "practical framework in which to deliver usage statistics" for licensed electronic information resources.[1] Minimum requirements are addressed as well as the kinds of database elements that should be available, such as the number of sessions, queries, menu selections, and full-content units. Sample report formats with minimum data requirements are available. With this model, the number of sessions and the number of queries would provide comparative usage statistics. In the *Code of Practice,* COUNTER provides definitions and standardizes usage statistics for librarians and vendors. Its aim is to promote an international standard for usage statistics.[2]

If all database vendors agreed to adhere to a standard, then usage statistics would be consistent from database to database and vendor to vendor. However, as of this date there has not been uniform acceptance by all vendors to provide standardized usage statistics. An alternative way to obtain consistent usage statistics is with Web analysis software. Such software is both commercially available and free. WebTrends Log Analyzer, 123 LogAnalyzer, and Analog are a few examples. This method requires that a program be installed on a server that records users' access to databases in a log file and analyzes Web site activity. Not all libraries have the software or the expertise to implement it, so; they depend on the statistics provided by the database vendors. When this is the case, identify statistics provided by each vendor that represent the total number of times access to the database occurred or total number of sessions. Calculate the cost per use by dividing the total number of sessions into the cost of the database for the same time.

When budget allocations are a motivating factor for conducting the evaluation, cost and use are valid markers by which to categorize databases. To categorize the databases in this manner, determine the median cost and use for all of the databases evaluated. Databases below the median are low-cost or low-use databases, and databases above the median are high-cost or high-use databases. Identify each database by one of the following: low cost/low use, high cost/high use, low cost/high use, and high cost/low use. Databases that fall within the high-cost/low-use category become priorities for the evaluation process (see Table 3.1).

Gathering data about journal titles enables the library to identify and compare duplicated and unique titles. Create a comparative list of journal titles by obtaining a list of titles from the journal directory in each database. The example in Exhibit 3.2 compares journal titles

TABLE 3.1. Cost per use analysis.

Database name	Cost	Use	Cost/use	Comments
Database 1	LC	LU	LC/LU	
Database 2	HC	HU	HC/HU	
Database 3	LC	HU	LC/HU	
Database 4	HC	LU	HC/LU	

EXHIBIT 3.2. Journal Title Comparisons

Art index full text	Humanities index full text
African Arts	*African Arts*
Afterimage	
American Cinematographer	
	American Drama
	American Indian Culture and Research Journal
	The American Indian Quarterly
	American Jewish History
	American Journalism
	American Journalism Review
	The American Poetry Review
	The American Scholar
	American Studies International
	ANQ
Animation Magazine	
	The Antioch Review
Antiquity	*Antiquity*
Aperture	
Architecture	
Archivo Español de Arte	
Art & Antiques	
	The Art Bulletin
Art Bulletin of Nationalmuseum Stockholm	
Art Business News	
Art Criticism	
American Visions	
Applied Arts	
Architectural Digest	
Ars Orientalis	
The Art Bulletin	
Art Issues	
Art Journal	*Art Journal*
Art Monthly	
Art New England	

(continued)

(continued)

Art index full text	**Humanities index full text**
Art Nexus	
Art Papers	
Art Press	
Art Review (London, England)	
Art/Text	
Arte Veneta	
Artext	
Arts & the Islamic World	
Arts d'Afrique Noire	
Artweek	
	Asian Folklore Studies
	Asian Perspectives
Assemblage	

starting with the letter "A" in Art Index and Humanities Index. The number of journal titles duplicated in Art Index compared with Humanities Index is three of thirty-three titles, a 9 percent duplication rate; the number of titles duplicated in Humanities Index compared with Art Index is three of eighteen titles, or 18 percent. Databases that have a duplication rate of at least 50 percent should be marked for further, analysis. A journal duplication rate of less than 50 percent is reasonable depending on the types of databases; however, the acceptable rate of duplication should be determined by the library.

A new service, Overlap Analysis, offered by Serials Solutions provides database journal analysis. The results include unique journals, overlap journals, total journals, and percent unique.[3] Automation of this process by a vendor allows for more precise, in-depth analysis of unique and duplicated journal titles in a collection.

Libraries often compare themselves with peer institutions as well as institutions they aspire to emulate. Any library going through this evaluation process may elect to include database comparisons of peer institutions, or peer comparisons, as additional information for the evaluators.

Although use is not quantifiable when evaluating a trial database, if the trial database is a potential replacement for an existing database then it is feasible to evaluate both databases concurrently. For example, if the library subscribes to a database that has a search interface that is difficult to use and a trial for another database with comparable content is available, consider evaluating both databases. It may become evident which search engine and user interface is more user friendly. Points to consider include familiarity with a particular search interface, provision of a more consistent search environment, and improved ease of use. In addition, evaluating trial databases is an opportune time to query various library populations; input from students, faculty, and librarians will provide different perspectives. Thus, the question becomes which database users prefer. The evaluation forms are customizable to suit the needs of each population, and the evaluative part of the process indicates user preferences.

Team leaders will assemble, compile, and complete the known data on the evaluation form and distribute copies, along with the Journal Title Comparisons, to the evaluators. With the data in hand, the evaluators are ready to evaluate the databases and rank the content, unique content, ease of use, instruction, and overall quality. Observations and remarks are appropriate to include as Comments. When the deadline arrives, the team leaders will collect the evaluation forms and proceed to the next phase, which is to collate, analyze, and interpret the data.

PHASE III

In the last phase of the evaluation process, the team leaders establish a final ranking for each database by calculating the mean of each criterion from the returned forms and then calculating the total mean for each database. Determine the need score by assigning a numeric value to each descriptor and calculating the average. The team leaders can summarize the data (see Table 3.2), present the results, and lead group discussions. Based on the results of this process, recommendations and final decisions about the disposition of the databases are made.

A CASE STUDY

At the University of Montevallo, the librarians deemed it appropriate to review all of the databases in anticipation of continuing budget pressures. Because many databases were available at no charge via a statewide consortium, the librarians wanted to be sure that the institution did not pay for any

TABLE 3.2. Data summary.

Database	Cost	Use	Cost/use	Duplication (50 percent)	Peer comparisons	Evaluations (0-4)	Need

Comments:

databases that were content redundant. It was determined that the library would carefully examine, and potentially eliminate, any databases that were high cost/low use or that duplicated journal titles by 50 percent or more. The librarians agreed that retention of high-cost/low-use databases is valid only if justifiable reasons existed to retain them such as supporting the accreditation process of an academic program. In addition, potential controversy regarding database retention and weeding decisions based on personal preferences created the need to develop a collaborative process with objective results.

The first phase of the process included determining which criteria were important to include on the evaluation form, grouping databases by subjects, and assigning team leaders to database categories based on the equitable distribution of the databases. Due dates and team leaders kept the process moving and on schedule (see Table 3.3).

The next phase, data collection, was labor-intensive but yielded a basic core of information: cost, use, and cost per use. Several librarians were responsible for gathering the known data determined by obvious job responsibilities; the library director was responsible for the cost data, the systems

TABLE 3.3. Database groupings.

Team leader 1 [Due date]	Team leader 2 [Due date]	Team leader 3 [Due date]	Team leader 4 [Due date]	Team leader 5 [Due date]
Business, careers	Education, psychology, social science, K-12	Literature, fine arts, humanities, encyclopedias	General, reference, other	Science, medical, other
Acxiom Biz	Contemporary Women's Issues	African American History & Culture	Academic Search Elite	Access Science
Acxiom Home	EBSCO Animals	Art Abs	AP Photo Archive	ACS Web Editions
Buckmaster Annual Reports	Education Abstracts	Arts & Humanities Search	Article First	Agricola
Business & Company Resource Center	Electric Library	BGMI	Contents First	Applied Science & Technology Abs
Business & Industry	ERIC (AVL)	Biography Index	Data Times	Basic Biosis
Business & Management Practices	ERIC (First Search)	Book Review Digest	Dissertations	Bio Ag Index
Business Dateline	ERIC full text	Books in Print (FS)	Emerald	Bio Digest
Business Organizations	Junior Quest	Books in Print Online	Expanded Academic ASAP	CINAHL
Business Source Elite	Kid Quest	Britannica Online	Fact Search	Clinical Reference Systems
Career & Technical Education	Legal Periodicals Index	Contemporary Authors	GPO	Event Line
College Source	Library Lit	Encyclopedia Americana	MAS Full Text Ultra	General Science Abs
Consumer Index	LLBA	Ethnic News Watch	MasterFile Premier	GEOBASE
Disclosure	Mental Measurements Yearbook	Funk & Wagnall's New World Encyclopedia	Newspaper Abstracts	Health Source Plus

TABLE 3.3 *(continued)*

Team leader 1 [Due date]	Team leader 2 [Due date]	Team leader 3 [Due date]	Team leader 4 [Due date]	Team leader 5 [Due date]
Business, careers	Education, psychology, social science, K-12	Literature, fine arts, humanities, encyclopedias	General, reference, other	Science, medical, other
EconLit	Middle Search Plus	Grangers World Poetry Online	Newspaper Source	MathSciNet
FIS Online	PAIS	Grolier	Periodicals Abstracts	MDX Health
General Business ASAP	Primary Search	Humanities Abs	Periodicals Abstracts Research II	MEDLINE
Internet & Personal Computing Abs	Professional Development Collection	MLA Bibliography	PQ Gold Periodicals	Net First
S&P Net Advantage	PsycFirst	Music Literature (RILM)	PQ Reference	Papers First
Stat USA	PsycInfo	Oxford English Dictionary	ProQuest Newspapers	Proceedings
Vocational Search	SIRS (2 vendors)	Poem Finder	Readers Guide Abs	Serials Directory
Wall Street Journal	Social Science Abs	Scribner's Writers Series	Union List of Periodicals	STN Chemical Abstracts
Wilson Business	Sports Discus	Twaynes World Authors	Wilson Select Plus	Ulrichs
World Scope	Teacher Journals	World Book (2 vendors)	World Almanac	USP DI Vol II, Advice for the Patient
			World Cat	

librarian was responsible for usage data and calculating cost per use, and the collection development librarian was responsible for compiling journal title comparisons. Later, the instruction librarians requested the addition of peer comparisons. The team leaders coordinated their efforts with these librarians to pull the data together and distributed the evaluation forms with the known data completed on the forms. Each librarian reviewed the information, searched the databases, and completed the evaluation section of the form. Shared searches, search strategies, and database discoveries became topics of conversation.

When the due dates arrived, the team leaders gathered the evaluation forms, compiled and distributed the results, and led the discussion in which the librarians determined the disposition of the databases. The ranking system enabled the team leaders to present the numerical results in an objective manner. Identified for further analysis and discussion were databases above or below the median in any of these categories: cost, use, duplication, evaluations, and need. The desired results included low cost, high use, low duplication, high evaluations, and a need rating of useful or essential. Therefore, any database with high cost, low use, high duplication, low evaluations, and a need score of "inappropriate" were questionable (see Table 3.4). Using these results, expositive discussions led to database retention and weeding decisions.

TABLE 3.4. Results—Team leader 5.

Databases	Cost	Use	Duplication	Evaluations	Need
Science					
ASTI	.62	1	OK	3.6	Inappropriate
BasicBiosis	22.32	36	69.8%	4.2	Essential
BioAgIndex	22.32	36	50%	3.6	Useful
EventLine	0	0	NCD	3.3	Inappropriate
Gen Science	25.42	41	52%	4.2	Useful
Medical					
MDX Health	0	0	40%	3.5	Inappropriate
Other					
Ulrich's	618	78	250,000 titles	3.9	Useful

Duplication: OK if 50 percent; NCD = no comparable data.
Evaluations: Based on 0-5 rating scale.

During the initial process, difficulties encountered included gathering the known data, investing of time, staying on task, and maintaining a project focus. With this in mind, several changes were made. The evaluation process became electronic, simultaneous evaluation of a limited number of databases occurred, and the rating scale was revised. These changes enabled a more efficient process with greater participation.

ELECTRONIC APPLICATION OF THE EVALUATION PROCESS

Initial distribution of the evaluation forms and collation of the results was done manually but evolved into an electronic process, enabling easier access to the evaluation forms and greater participation by multiple user groups. When the process is electronic, evaluators access the evaluation form from a Web page on the library site and the database from a URL on the form. A pop-up window provides access to the database and to the evaluation form simultaneously.

Once set up, electronic access is easier for distribution, evaluation, and collation of the data. Customized to suit the needs of the target population, tailored evaluation forms provide database information appropriate for each user group. After the evaluative criteria are established and the format determined, usability studies further refined the evaluation instrument. Faculty provided feedback regarding use of the form and identified items that needed further clarification. Several examples of Web-based evaluation forms with varying degrees of modifications based on the objective of the evaluation and on the target population follow are shown in Exhibits 3.3 through 3.6.

Instructions are at the top of each form. Excluded on the Student Evaluation Form is "Known Data." "Instruction" was changed to "Assignment use," and the evaluator's name was eliminated to provide anonymity (see Exhibit 3.3). Conversely, the Faculty Evaluation Form included "Known Data" (see Exhibit 3.4). Evaluation forms can be for single or multiple databases (see Exhibit 3.5) as well as for databases currently subscribed to or available on a trial basis (see Exhibit 3.6). In this case, cost depends on the number of institutions that will participate in a consortium agreement; therefore, cost and use are not included on the form for a trial database.

After the forms were completed, the evaluators submitted them. The results were automatically compiled in an Access database

EXHIBIT 3.3. Student Evaluation Form

Please complete and submit this form. Access the database by clicking on the name of the database.

Database name: BioOne

Content: ○0 ○1 ○2 ○3 ○4
Unique content: ○0 ○1 ○2 ○3 ○4
Ease of use: ○0 ○1 ○2 ○3 ○4
Assignment use: ○0 ○1 ○2 ○3 ○4
Overall quality: ○0 ○1 ○2 ○3 ○4

0 = Inappropriate 1 = Very Unsatisfactory 2 = Unsatisfactory
3 = Satisfactory 4 = Very Satisfactory

Need: _____ Inappropriate _____ Useful _____ Essential

Comments:

EXHIBIT 3.4. Faculty Evaluation Form

Please complete and submit this form. Access the database by clicking on the name of the database.

Database name: BioOne

Known Data

Cost: $1,559
Use: 246
Cost/use: $6.34
Peer comparisons: 5 out of 17 COPLAC institutions

Evaluations

Content: ○0 ○1 ○2 ○3 ○4
Unique content: ○0 ○1 ○2 ○3 ○4
Ease of use: ○0 ○1 ○2 ○3 ○4
Assignment use: ○0 ○1 ○2 ○3 ○4
Overall quality: ○0 ○1 ○2 ○3 ○4

0 = Inappropriate 1 = Very Unsatisfactory 2 = Unsatisfactory
3 = Satisfactory 4 = Very Satisfactory

Need: _____ Inappropriate _____ Useful _____ Essential

Comments:

EXHIBIT 3.5. Faculty Evaluation Form
for Multiple Databases

Please complete and submit one form for each database by clicking on a radio button. Access the database by clicking on the name of the database.

Database name: ○BioOne   ○SportsDiscus ○RILM   ○MathSciNet

Known Data

Cost, use, and cost/use from 2003 statistics.

Database	BioOne	SportsDiscus	RILM	MathSciNet
Cost	$1,871.00	$1,750.00	$1,376.50	$405.00
Use	300	240	85	157
Cost/use	$ 6.24	$ 7.29	$ 16.19	$ 2.58
Duplication/ coverage	12 of 71 titles are duplicated	Indexes 23 of 34 kinesiology journals	Indexes all music journals	Covers mathematical reviews and current mathematical publications
Peer com- parisons	5 out of 17 COPLAC institutions	5 out of 17 COPLAC institutions	5 out of 17 COPLAC institutions	10 out of 15 COPLAC institutions

Evaluations

Content: ○0   ○1   ○2   ○3   ○4
Unique content: ○0   ○1   ○2   ○3   ○4
Ease of use: ○0   ○1   ○2   ○3   ○4
Assignment use: ○0   ○1   ○2   ○3   ○4
Overall quality: ○0   ○1   ○2   ○3   ○4

0 = Inappropriate 1 = Very Unsatisfactory 2 = Unsatisfactory
3 = Satisfactory 4 = Very Satisfactory

Need: _____ Inappropriate   _____ Useful   _____ Essential

Comments:

**EXHIBIT 3.6. Librarian Evaluation Form
for Multiple Trial Databases**

Please complete and submit one form for each database. Access the database by clicking on the name of the database. Passwords are available via e-mail.

Database name:	⭕Westlaw	⭕Access Archives	⭕Cambridge Scientific	⭕Facts on File

Evaluations

Content:	⭕0	⭕1	⭕2	⭕3	⭕4
Unique content:	⭕0	⭕1	⭕2	⭕3	⭕4
Ease of use:	⭕0	⭕1	⭕2	⭕3	⭕4
Assignment use:	⭕0	⭕1	⭕2	⭕3	⭕4
Overall quality:	⭕0	⭕1	⭕2	⭕3	⭕4

0 = Inappropriate 1 = Very Unsatisfactory 2 = Unsatisfactory
3 = Satisfactory 4 = Very Satisfactory

Need: _____ Inappropriate _____ Useful _____ Essential

Comments:

(see Table 3.5). Conversion from Access to Excel and calculation of the average in an Excel spreadsheet determined the final score, or rating, of each database (see Table 3.6). At this point, the results are available for distribution and discussion.

With this process, database purchase and retention decisions become logical and straightforward and are founded on a numerical analysis, which is less subjective. Customization of the process establishes a mechanism to evaluate a variety of databases with numerous user populations and enables justified purchase decisions. Thus, the application of this methodology for the assessment of one database, or a collection of databases, for acquisition, retention, and withdrawal purposes provides a collaborative experience with objective results.

TABLE 3.5. Results—Access database.

Database	Content	Unique content	Ease of use	Instruction	Overall quality	Need
Westlaw	2	3	2	1	2	Inappropriate
Accessible Archives	1	2	0	0	0	Inappropriate
Cambridge Scientific	3	1	1	1	1	Inappropriate
Facts on File	1	1	2	2	1	Inappropriate
Facts on File	3	2	2	3	2	Useful
Accessible Archives	3	4	3	3	3	Useful
Westlaw	3	3	2	2	3	Useful
Accessible Archives	3	4	2	2	2	Inappropriate
Cambridge Scientific	4	3	2	2	3	Useful
Accessible Archives	3	4	3	3	3	Useful
Cambridge Scientific	4	4	4	4	4	Essential
Facts on File	4	4	4	4	4	Essential
Cambridge Scientific	4	4	3	3	3	Useful
Westlaw	3	2	2	2	2	Inappropriate
Westlaw	3	4	3	3	3	Useful
Accessible Archives	3	3	3	3	3	Useful
Cambridge Scientific	3	4	3	3	3	Useful

TABLE 3.5 *(continued)*

Database	Content	Unique content	Ease of use	Instruction	Overall quality	Need
Facts on File	3	4	3	3	3	Useful
Westlaw	3	3	0	0	2	Inappropriate
Facts on File	0	0	0	0	0	Inappropriate

TABLE 3.6. Results—Excel spreadsheet.

Database	Content	Unique content	Ease of use	Instruction	Overall quality	Need
Accessible Archives	1	2	0	0	0	Inappropriate
	3	4	3	3	3	Useful
	3	4	2	2	2	Inappropriate
	3	4	3	3	3	Useful
	3	3	3	3	3	Useful
Results	2.60	3.40	2.20	2.20	2.20	2.52
Cambridge Scientific	3	1	1	1	1	Inappropriate
	4	3	2	2	3	Useful
	4	4	4	4	4	Essential
	4	4	3	3	3	Useful
	3	4	3	3	3	Useful
Results	3.60	3.20	2.60	2.60	2.80	2.96
Facts on File	1	1	2	2	1	Inappropriate
	3	2	2	3	2	Useful
	4	4	4	4	4	Essential
	3	4	3	3	3	Useful

TABLE 3.6 *(continued)*

Database	Content	Unique content	Ease of use	Instruction	Overall quality	Need
	0	0	0	0	0	Inappropriate
Results	2.20	2.20	2.20	2.40	2.00	2.20
Westlaw	2	3	2	1	2	Inappropriate
	3	3	2	2	3	Useful
	3	2	2	2	2	Inappropriate
	3	4	3	3	3	Useful
	3	3	0	0	2	Inappropriate
Results	2.80	3.00	1.80	1.60	2.40	2.32

NOTES

1. International Coalition of Library Consortia (ICOLC). *Statements and Documents of the International Coalition of Library Consortia (ICOLC): Guidelines for Statistical Measures of Usage of Web-Based Information Resources, December 2001.* http://www.library.yale.edu/consortia/2001webstats.htm. December 12, 2003.

2. Counter Online Metrics. *COUNTER—Counting Online Usage of Networked Electronic Resources,* 10 October 2003. http://www.projectcounter.org/. May 19, 2004.

3. Serials Solutions, Inc. *Overlap Analysis,* 24 May 2004. http://www.serialssolutions.com/overlap.asp. May 25, 2004.

Chapter 4

Collection Development Strategies for Online Aggregated Databases

Susan McMullen
Patricia B. M. Brennan
Joanna M. Burkhardt
Marla Wallace

A BRIEF HISTORY OF ELECTRONIC COLLECTION DEVELOPMENT

The 1989 Association of College & Research Libraries (ACRL) Clip Note #11, *Collection Development Policies for College Libraries,* listed only one example of a college library with a collection development policy for "special formats," specifically computer software. Technology has changed considerably, and the amount of library material available in an electronic format has increased exponentially since 1989. Collection development managers have been required to address this increased availability in the collection development policies for their institutions.

Selection of electronic products for the library has many of the hallmarks of the processes used for nonelectronic materials. Clayton and Gorman, Thornton, Holleman, and Metz suggest that products considered for acquisition should

- meet user needs;
- meet institutional goals, objectives, and priorities;
- comply with the institutional selection policy (which will address quality, relevance to the collection, and aesthetic aspects); and
- fit within the confines of the budget, balance the collection, and address resource sharing and cooperative development agreements.[1]

doi:10.1300/5580_04

Licensing, accessibility, hardware, archiving, format, copyright, and delivery of electronic products are issues specific to electronic products. Collection development policies must incorporate guidelines that speak to these product-specific questions.

COLLECTION DEVELOPMENT POLICIES
FOR ELECTRONIC RESOURCES

There is general agreement among those who write on the subject that a detailed collection development/acquisition policy for the institution in question is essential. Existing policies require updating on a regular basis and as technology and equipment change. The specific issues relating to electronic products can be incorporated into existing guidelines, added as a separate set of guidelines to the existing document, or written as a separate policy specific to electronic products.

Many institutions have made their collection development policies accessible via the World Wide Web. A useful list of institutions and the Web links to their collection development policies has been posted by Anne Okerson of Yale University at http://www.library.yale.edu/~okerson/ecd.html.

In examining some of these policies, a variety of approaches can be found. Some institutions (including University of Notre Dame, Monash University of Australia, and Dartmouth College) do not have a separate policy for electronic materials, perhaps indicating that this practice is an issue of format and does not impact on collection development per se. Some, such as Columbia University and Boston Public Library, list specific criteria for consideration when electronic format is an option, perhaps indicating that the format might have some impact on the collection development decision. Several institutions have a separate policy for collection of electronic materials when they are being considered for acquisition. University of North Carolina at Asheville, University of Oregon, University of New Orleans, University of Minnesota, University of Wyoming, and University of Tennessee, Knoxville, all have separate policies for electronic acquisitions. Yale is among the institutions that have one policy for materials purchased alone and another for electronic materials purchased consortially.

In Patricia Bril's chapter on consortial collection development in *Collection Management in Academic Libraries,* she indicated that patrons use the "law of least effort," meaning that they seek convenience of access before quality of results.[2] In 1991, when this book was published, Bril mentioned that consortial buying and sharing of electronic materials would have to wait until computers became more standardized. At that time most of the efforts at shared collection development between or among institutions had failed. However, in today's electronic environment, library users now opt for electronic access over a physical visit to the library. The standardized technology now exists to the extent that consortial purchase and use of electronic databases and other tools is not only possible, but in some cases preferable.

The policy for selection and acquisition of electronic products should address the criteria listed previously. However, the special features and requirements of electronic products demand additional guidelines. Electronic products come in many forms. Some are simply replicas of the paper version. They are the exact equivalent of the paper version but in an electronic format. Some will have the text plus added capabilities such as search, data manipulation, or alerting. Still others will include text plus high-tech features such as hypermedia, electronic analog models, motion, and sound.

It is still very important to consider the capabilities of the electronic product in relation to the capabilities of the hardware available. If the product requires more computer power or memory than is widely available, the product will not be a useful addition to the collection.

Collection policies should also consider single-user versus multi-user access, speed and functionality of the product, content—including the way(s) in which full text is made available—archiving and long-term access, links, the user interface, connection files, special features, authentication, remote versus local use, bundling with other products or stand-alone, duplication of information in other formats, competing products, one-time purchase versus subscription, stability of the provider, technical support, and fluidity of contents. Many of these issues are discussed in this chapter.

AGGREGATORS

What is an aggregator database? A sweep across the literature of librarianship, publishing, and various academic disciplines shows that the term can be and has been used in many contexts, including the following:

- Weblog/blog news summarizers such as Syndic8 and NewsIsFree
- Market research gateways such as MindBranch
- Permanent journal archive projects, or what Li and Leung call "stable aggregators," such as JSTOR or Project MUSE[3]
- Abstracting and indexing services that contain or are linked to full-text material—or what Li and Leung call "unstable aggregators," such as databases from EBSCOhost and ProQuest

This overview focuses on the issues surrounding the creation and development of the "unstable aggregators." First, however, a review of the history of aggregator databases is in order.

HISTORY OF AGGREGATOR DATABASES

In the glory days of the CD-ROM revolution, before the rapid rise of the public Internet, and long before the creation of the Web, University Microfilms Inc. (UMI) was the dominant, one might almost say exclusive, creator and distributor of periodical and newspaper backfiles for libraries. UMI realized that it possessed a potential gold mine. Periodical indices on CD-ROM had gained some level of acceptance by libraries of all types. What if actual article images could be linked to a powerful aggregation of indexes to give users access to, instead of mere awareness of, the contents of hundreds of periodical publications? Enter ProQuest. According to the announcement following its debut at the American Library Association meeting in June 1990, "'ProQuest' is the new name for UMI's family of CD-ROM products. It will apply to UMI's current line of [CD-ROM] databases, and any subsequent database and hardware offerings."[4] Little did anyone realize at the time what momentous changes that first aggregator "banner" would weather. Within six months, vendors were offering CD-ROM minichangers—or towers—with almost 4 gigabytes of online storage to accommodate the increasing amount of direct content offered with CD-ROM-based periodical indexing. By late 1992, *Library Journal* published a comparative review of four periodical indices with accompanying article content on CD-ROM: EBSCO Magazine Article Summaries Full Text Elite, InfoTrac Magazines ASAP Plus, ProQuest Magazine Express, and Wilson Readers' Guide Abstracts and Readers' Guide Select Edition.[5] These major aggregators went head to head in 1992, and they continue to do so today.

However, these products focus coverage on "magazines." Generalist periodical literature of the type librarians have always associated with *Wilsons' Readers' Guide to Periodical Literature* made these products extremely attractive to large, well-funded public libraries but only moderately interesting to academic libraries. At the next level of sophistication, aggregations of business periodicals appeared on CD-ROM almost simultaneously with their more generalist cousins—a bit more interesting to college and university libraries with established curricula in these areas. The vendors, however, were not yet grappling with the scholarly journals and periodicals that are the lifeblood of the academic library. They also were not yet prepared to address many of the issues that flow from the library's academic mission to support permanent, complete access to particular publications or bodies of literature.

ACADEMIC LIBRARIES
AND ELECTRONIC JOURNALS

The purposes and aims of popular magazine publishing and scholarly journal publishing are fundamentally different. Magazines exist to make money for their publishers by filling a market niche, providing a service, advancing a cause, or publicizing a sociopolitical point of view. Christopher L. Tomlins (editor of *Law and History Review,* the journal of the American Society for Legal History), in a wonderfully cogent paper, republished by the American Council of Learned Societies, writes:

> Scholarly journals . . . are created to be disseminators of authoritative scholarship—authoritative in three senses. First, authoritative in the sense that the scholarship the journal publishes is certified by its editorial practices to be as reliable as the collective expertise of the group of professionals who have produced and judged the scholarship can make it (a group that encompasses originating author, editor, referees, copy editor, managing editor, typesetter, production manager, et al.). Second, authoritative in that the journal represents authored knowledge, knowledge that is definitively attributable, that has achieved a unique representation for which an author and an editorial process is answerable and is identifiably responsible, knowledge that is substantively stable and will not alter without becoming something identifiably

different, as in differently authored, or differently attributable—
and if thus altered, then altered in accordance with defensible
and acceptable and reasonable professional canons of what dif-
ference constitutes. Third, authoritative in the sense of authorized for inclusion in an archive, for that is what a scholarly
journal also is.[6]

Having brought the perspective of the academy, particularly as it
applies to the humanities and social sciences, as well as the point of
view of the editor of a well-regarded but small academic journal to
this view of the scholarly journal, Tomlins goes on to capture the
counterbalanced threats and opportunities of electronic publishing
for scholarly journals at the cusp of the twenty-first century. Outside
the academy, many of those involved in the actual electronic dissemination or distribution of scholarly journal contents—and therefore involved in determining their future in the online environment—view
academic journals as "bundles of resources, mobilized in the rapid
commodification of information that dominates [our] culture." Pro-
ponents of this view include "publishers, aggregators, information
services, and their institutional clients."[7]

AGGREGATORS' IMPACT ON COLLECTION
DEVELOPMENT DECISIONS

By the early to mid-1990s, the increasing sophistication of the public
Internet, followed by the advent of the World Wide Web, spread both
the benefits and the pitfalls of electronic publishing. The need to extend the reach of the useful and accurate as a counterbalance "between the traditionally sanctioned and well-funded . . . the unfunded
and unsanctioned . . . or lone lunatic"[8] propelled many publishers of
academic journals to find ways to make their material accessible electronically. Many avenues were explored, and many of those avenues
remain well traveled, from free access to the same material published
in paper (e.g., *Proceedings of the National Academy of Sciences*—
PNAS), to cover-to-cover reproduction and archiving of specific
groups of titles (e.g., JSTOR and Project MUSE), to direct access by
subscription to a publisher-maintained Web site, to loading of content
in "unstable aggregators." However, aggregation has frequently inter-
fered with, or failed to maintain, the sense of authority so valued by

the college and university. Instead, it emphasized the commodity value of individual pieces of information to individual users. The bundling, or aggregation, of large numbers of journal titles, based principally on current availability of content by publisher contract, often led to the unwitting "acquisition"—however temporary—of titles that a library would not have considered acquiring by individual subscription. The enthusiasm of the library community for the astounding availability of so much digital content—from a small group of aggregated titles on CD-ROM fifteen years ago, to a few hundred aggregated titles on CD-ROM in the early 1990s, to hundreds of aggregated titles via telnet on the Internet, to thousands of aggregated titles via the World Wide Web—led to some instances of uncritical collection development decisions.

Assuming that once content was included, access to it would remain stable, some libraries withdrew or deaccessioned titles included in aggregator databases only to discover that publisher contracts were fluid and that content could be added or withdrawn by the publisher or aggregator at any time. The library was renting—not buying.

The effects of these collection development decisions are highly dependent on the importance attached to particular periodicals by individual academic communities. One institution's vital publication is another's secondary purchase or irrelevant title. Although some libraries found themselves scrambling to reassemble in physical form or through direct electronic subscription materials that they had previously withdrawn, most had cautiously continued to hold the most valued titles in physical form as the electronic publishing landscape began to offer more stable choices for archived electronic versions of those journals. Yet as recently as 2000, Reich and Rosenthal, writing for Highwire Press at Stanford, noted:

> Librarians have an equally well-founded skepticism that they can provide their readers with long-term access to material published on the Web. Important content can be changed or removed at the publisher's whim. It is leased to subscribers; they don't own it. There is no local "collection" for a library to develop or manage. The publisher's promise of "perpetual access" is empty, there is no enforcement mechanism behind it. The result is that libraries are reluctant to subscribe to Web journals.[9]

This skepticism was born out as recently as 2003, when Sage Publications withdrew its prestigious social sciences journal content not only from various aggregators but also from the Online Computer Library Center (OCLC) Electronic Collections Online—whose mission it is to permanently archive content for institutional subscribers.

Although some parts of the user community—typically undergraduate students—would like to see the electronic format replace physical access as quickly as possible, other parts of the academic community will continue to rely on librarians' prudence, caution, thorough knowledge of the library's user community and its curricular emphases, as well as forward-thinking to inform decisions about the library's periodical "collection."

> The online environment is not the wave of the future, it is the wave of the present. . . .[10] [I]n an information environment that is already highly commodified and becoming daily ever more so . . . [there is] no doubt that to continue to play its first, preferred role of scholarly authorizer, the journal will have to prove itself attractive as a player in the second incarnation too, as a supplier fit to be included in the commodification of information.[11]

To this end, academic publishers continue to offer their content to aggregator databases, and academic librarians continue to influence aggregators to become cognizant of and attempt to address those issues of continuing importance to the academic community—continuity of access, completeness of coverage, and stability of the backfile.

EVALUATING DATABASE CONTENT AND FEATURES

In choosing an aggregator database, libraries need to decide which features are most crucial to their users and develop a methodology for evaluating these features. It is useful first to develop a list of guidelines concerning database functionality. Which features are of primary importance to your library, which are marginal, and which can provide value-added services? Areas that require particular analysis include the following:

- Breadth and depth of coverage
- Quality of indexing

- Usability, which includes screen design and ease of searching
- Ability to customize the database
- Delivery options
- Accessibility
- Availability of statistical usage data
- Quality of support

Breadth and Depth of Coverage

What is the content of the database? Evaluating database content goes well beyond such preliminary indicators as quantity of titles indexed and numbers of full-text journals included. The value of a full-text database greatly depends on its ability to offer additional quality sources to the library's collection that otherwise may be beyond the reach of its serials acquisitions budget. Consequently, librarians should be examining the full-text titles contained within a database to determine how many are peer reviewed. Of the peer-reviewed journals included, how many are unique or exclusive to a particular database? Another indication of database content value is how the database is evolving over time. Over the past year, how many scholarly journals have been added compared with how many have been halted or removed? Look at the same statistics over a two-year and three-year time frame as well.[12] Can you discern any trends in the direction of database content? What are the dates of coverage for each title? How is the vendor handling cessations? If a publication is halted or removed, how is the customer notified? Is it easy to tell which titles have been halted or removed? Are archival issues still available within the database or have they been eliminated? Is indexing to these previously full-text journals still provided?

In their study, Brier and Lebbin stressed the importance of evaluating title coverage of full-text databases in relation to the library's print collection. The database that provides the greatest number of titles may not necessarily provide the highest quality journals or the most appropriate titles for a particular library's collection needs or clientele.[13] Because the goal of an academic library is to provide more scholarly resources to the library's collection, a subject content analysis of peer-reviewed title coverage may also help librarians determine if a particular vendor's database content may add value to their subject journal collections. In addition, one might consider how many of the library's print and electronic subscriptions are indexed by the database, thus ensuring access to library-owned collections. Although this criterion is definitely a convenience, it is not an indication of the quality of titles indexed that would be available from other libraries through interlibrary loan.

Because of the ever-changing nature of publisher licensing for journal content in aggregator databases, librarians have to be concerned about the gaps that can occur in their collections when key publications are dropped from an aggregator's database. In a volatile marketplace, it is often risky to discontinue a print subscription solely because the item is available in an aggregator database. An example of this type of volatility occurred when Sage Publications removed their full-text journals from aggregator databases such as EBSCOHost and ProQuest and began selling them separately in "Sage Full-Text Collections." Each collection is currently individually licensed through Cambridge Scientific Abstracts.

Embargo periods lasting a year or longer have also made it more problematic for libraries to drop print subscriptions to journals whose current content is essential for research. An embargo is a publisher-imposed restriction that does not allow vendors to display full-text content from their journal titles for a defined period of time. An embargo period is meant to prevent libraries from canceling their print subscriptions just because they get the content electronically through an aggregator database.

Questions to ask vendors concerning embargo periods include the following:

- What percentage of their full-text journals have embargo periods?
- What are the specific titles of the journals with embargoes? Are they titles for which you need the latest twelve months of coverage or do you have print backups available?
- How easy is it to determine which journals have embargoes and what is their embargo period?
- Are embargo periods clearly stated on title lists, and are those title lists easily accessible online?

Another indicator of breadth and depth of coverage is the number of scholarly or peer-reviewed journals found within search results. "Search results that contain articles in the greatest number of scholarly journals may not always be found in databases with the largest journal count."[14]

Quality of Indexing

In their study completed in 1999, librarians from HELIN, the Rhode Island academic library consortium, wanted to define "electronic full-text content" really meant. What are the indexing criteria used by the major database vendors? Librarians compared actual print issues of several journal titles to the full-text content available within the database to determine how closely the online full-text or full-image content matched that of the print journal. "What the vendor calls full-text access may not mean cover-to-cover full-text access."[15] What type of content is provided? Substantial articles? Brief articles (less than a column in length)? Editorials? Commentary? Special issues? To do this type of evaluation, it is necessary to display online the contents of an individual issue. Being able to view the table of contents for a particular journal issue is also vitally important today as a means of tracking articles that have been cross-referenced from other databases or from the library's online catalog. When replacing paper subscriptions with online full-text access, librarians should be aware that they risk losing access not only to the entire title if the publisher pulls its content from the database, but, because of variations in indexing criteria and quality, to portions of varying lengths that may not be included or accessible by the aggregator.

The subject authority used to construct the database will have a clear impact on its search and retrieval functionality. Does the database use Library of Congress Subject Headings, or another standard thesaurus, or its own controlled vocabulary? What record fields are indexed and searchable? What fields are automatically included in a basic keyword search? Does the database support subject as well as keyword searching? Can a user browse by subject or view an online thesaurus? The availability of subheadings and related terms within a subject browse can be especially useful. Linked subject descriptors for each record are essential. Explore these links to determine the breadth and depth of subject indexing. Is the subject linking well developed, or does it capture only a portion of the articles that may be available on a subject in the database?

Another indexing consideration is the availability of information on title changes. Journals frequently change titles, often leaving users and librarians confused about which title is a continuation for which journal. Are there cross-references to the older title, or are the old and new titles handled as separate entries with no cross-references? If a Browse by Publication feature is available, a link giving a detailed history of the title and its variations with dates is very helpful.

Finally, librarians should be concerned about the currency of the indexing. How readily are citations loaded after receipt of publications? Is there a time lag between the loading of citations and the availability of full text? Are there restrictions, such as embargo periods, that govern how soon the full text is made available after the citations are loaded? If so, does the vendor provide this information within the product in a publication list or elsewhere?[16]

Usability: Screen Design and Ease of Searching

Ideally, vendors perform tests to ensure that their database is easy to search and navigate and to view on screen. Librarians should be particularly concerned about the intuitiveness of the search interface. To perform their own tests, librarians simply have to ask a few users to carry out selected searches to see how successful they are or to observe users in their own search processes. Note how search terms are entered and if satisfactory results are retrieved. No matter what the content of the database is, if a user cannot successfully navigate his or her way through the search and retrieval process, its viability is compromised.[17]

Although there is no substitute for an informed database searcher, each database should provide information on its particular method and include context-sensitive help screens. Search options should be readily apparent, and searching should be self-explanatory. For example, users might be provided drop-down menus that contain options for searching all of the words or any of the words or for the exact phrase.

Questions to ask about usability and ease of searching include the following:

- Is terminology clear and consistent throughout the search and retrieval process?
- Are icons and buttons labeled with words?
- Is the navigational scheme clearly understood? Are links to the search screen, results lists, marked items, etc., clearly recognizable?
- Does the results screen offer users options for improving their search results?

- Is it clear to users how to limit or expand their search results? Which limiters are supported?
- Are advanced search options readily available and easy to understand?
- How are search idiosyncrasies handled, such as hyphenated names and Spanish surnames?
- If zero hits are retrieved, are users redirected or given the proper syntax for improving their search? What automated error checks or redirects are available?
- What delivery options are available, and are they clearly recognizable and easy to use?

These questions reflect what experts such as Jakob Nielsen have established as usability heuristics for Web design.[18] Nielsen's ten critieria provide a standard for measuring the usability of Web-based databases.

1. *Visibility of system status (Where am I and where can I go next?):* Is it readily apparent to the user what to do upon entering the database? Are the options for searching readily available? Once citations are displayed, is it obvious how to obtain full text? Is it clear to the user what is happening when certain display options open multiple windows?
2. *Match the system and the real world:* Is terminology clear and understandable to the user?
3. *User control and freedom:* Is the user in control of the search process? Can he or she easily return to the search screen? Are options for refining searches given on the results screen?
4. *Consistency and standards:* Does the database follow standard conventions that are recognized across a variety of databases? For example, is an asterisk (*) used to represent truncation? Are search buttons labeled and located where the user would expect them to be?
5. *Error prevention:* What instructions does the user get for entering proper syntax to achieve the desired results?
6. *Recognition rather than recall:* Is the design of the interface intuitive enough for the user to know how to proceed without having to remember specific usage instructions?

7. *Flexibility and efficiency of use:* Is it easy for the user to move among search, display, and result screens? How easy is it to manipulate results? Can users download them easily into bibliographic management software?

8. *Aesthetic and minimalist design:* The interface should be clean, and it should be easy for users to understand search options. Instructions should be minimal and written for scanability.

9. *Assistance to recognize, diagnose, and recover from errors:* If a user does not retrieve expected results, is it clear to the user what has happened? What types of error checks are in place for improper syntax or zero hits?

10. *Help and documentation:* Is help readily available? Is it context sensitive? Is there a searchable index of help topics? Does the database have its own tutorial?

Search Capabilities

Under the category of search capabilities, evaluation criteria can include whether Boolean logic is supported, if both subject and keyword searching is available, and what advanced or complex searching techniques are provided. Users should be able to perform field-specific searches, use Boolean connectors and proximity operators, and perform ordered searching with parentheses. Beyond keyword searching, what additional types of searching are available? Is natural language searching supported, and, if so, does it produce reliable results? Can users browse contents by publication? This is often an important capability for users wishing to see what is available within a particular journal title. What types of search limiters and expanders are provided— can results be limited to peer-reviewed journals, by date, or by publication? Is limiting provided from within a search results screen, or must the user set limits before executing a search? Providing additional search features within results can also prove very beneficial to a user. The ability to "find articles like this one" helps users unfamiliar with linked subject headings to discover similar articles on a particular topic once they have found one that may be especially relevant to their needs. By cross-referencing and linking the author field, users can also find additional articles by the same author.

Results and Delivery Options

The biggest concerns when evaluating results and their delivery options are functionality and ease of use. How easy is it for the user to view and manipulate the results? The ability to select individual records to export into a marked records list should be clearly indicated and easy to perform. How long does the database retain the marked records before they are cleared? Do users have enough time to evaluate and mark long lists of citations without fear of losing the records before they are able to finish? When users select marked lists for downloading or e-mailing, is it clear whether the user will receive only a list of citations or also full text if available? Do users have a choice to download or e-mail just the citation records? Can they download results directly into a bibliographic management program?

Printing, downloading, and e-mailing of results should be standard options in any vendor's product. Most aggregators deliver full-image content in pdf format, which requires users to have or to download Adobe Acrobat Reader before viewing. Specialized database content providers may require the downloading of their own reader software. This can sometimes be cumbersome for the occasional user of the product. Even with standard pdf, users can experience difficulties interfacing with different software platforms. What version of Acrobat Reader is needed to open the pdf content within the database? Does it work equally well on Macs and PCs? Are special printer drivers required to print nonstandard fonts? Does full-image content display in the same window, or does it require opening a separate window? To e-mail full-image content, users should have an automatic means to send the article as an attachment. When only full-image content is available, the default delivery method should be this attachment option.

Customization

Recognizing that libraries have unique collections and patrons, a vendor can greatly enhance a database's viability by making it customizable. An adaptable database allows librarians to tailor certain features and default screens to the skills and preferences of its clientele. For example, many librarians may wish to make a database's advanced search screen the default search interface. By working with a visual presentation of separate search boxes with options for Boolean connectors, many librarians feel that patrons will achieve better results. Librarians at other institutions may find that the advanced search screen is too confusing for their patrons, and they may prefer a more simplistic, single search box interact that defaults to an "and" search.

Other search customization options include the following:

- How much of the backfile to search automatically—all of it? The current year? Past three years?
- The ability to search all vendor-subscribed databases simultaneously, individually, or by subject area.
- The ability to choose search limiters and expanders.
- The decision to include links to vendor-evaluated Web resources in the search results.

Result display screens should also be customizable. At the most basic level, choices for displaying results might include how many citations are shown on a screen or how the results are sorted (i.e., by date or by relevance). When full-image content is displayed in pdf format, is there an option for showing it in the same window or opening up in a separate window? Results may be further customized to include a link to the library's online public access catalog (OPAC) or to a note about local holdings. Is cross-linking to other full-text databases and e-journal collections available? If so, should links be made available to these other collections? Librarians may wish to ask themselves how useful these links may be if they must appear in all title results. Is there a way to customize which links to other e-journal collections appear with which journal titles?

Branding the database with the library logo and with a link back to its home page can also be an effective marketing tool. This type of branding can send a message to users that the database contents are being offered by the library and are customized for their individual use.

Value-Added Features

As mentioned previously, cross linking among databases is a powerful way for users to find full-text resources outside of the database they are searching. How sophisticated is the level of cross-linking within the database? At its most basic, the database should link to the library's OPAC. The OPAC should in turn provide information on the library's holdings as well as links to online full-text title content from a variety of vendors. To provide this type of linking, vendors need to supply libraries with machine-readable cataloging (MARC)-formatted title records to be integrated into the library's catalog. Consequently, other criteria for evaluation would be to determine if MARC records are available and how extensive they are. What other types of cross-linking between database products are provided? Are database cross-links available only to some vendor-subscribed databases?

Other value-added features to consider include the following:

- Can users set up subject or search profiles so that they can be notified when new content becomes available in the database based on their subject interest or on a particular saved search?[19]
- Does the vendor supply consistent uniform resource locators (URLs) that can be included on library-produced course guides, instructor syllabi, or other Web-enabled instruction venues?
- Can results be downloaded into a bibliographic management databases such as EndNote or RefWorks? How cumbersome is this download process?

Accessibility and Customer Support

Library users are increasingly accessing database content from remote locations. Librarians need to be concerned with authenticating their users for access to these expensive database products. How are users authenticated? Does your library proxy server interface seamlessly with the database? How many user logins does your license allow? For general aggregator databases, a site license with unlimited logins is the standard.

With so many users accessing databases from outside of the library building, the need for enhanced help screens and other forms of customer support is also increased. Is the help feature context sensitive? How usable and complete is the index to the help contents—and are the contents searchable?

Usage Statistics

Although sometimes overlooked during the evaluation process, the availability and accessibility of usage statistics are very important components of the database. The reporting of usage statistics from database vendors is essential for library decision making and for validating the continued budgetary commitment for online database products. Usage statistics should provide librarians with enough information to analyze costs accurately, justify expenditures, and determine usage trends over time. Usage indicators can include a count of sessions, time per session, a count of searches, and a count of full-text downloads.

> In addition, usage statistics can show a variety of information, including success or failure of user access (e.g., turn-aways per time period per specific database), user access methods (e.g., telnet vs. browsers), access levels at one institution compared against peer institutions, cost of access (e.g., cost per downloaded item) and other items pertaining to user behaviors.[20]

When looking specifically at aggregator databases that supply the full text of many journal titles, it would be useful to know the number of full-text article downloads provided from each journal. This is particularly useful for cost analysis, allowing comparison of the actual cost per article download against the cost of the print subscription.

When evaluating networked databases, librarians should ensure that usage statistics will be provided on a regular and consistent basis. Are usage statistics continually available on a vendor's Web site, or do you have to wait for monthly, quarterly, or even annual reports? How will the data be distributed—by e-mail, fax, U.S. mail, or via the vendor's administrative Web site? Is the data automatically distributed or does it have to be requested? What about statistics in a consortial arrangement—can vendors successfully sort usage statistics to provide individualized reports to each institution in the consortium? When viewing statistics from a vendor's Web site, is there a choice of viewing formats? Some of the most common formats include Excel, pdf, csv, zip, and html. Librarians should look for usage reports that are easy to retrieve, manipulate, and interpret. Think about what is most convenient for your institution. Text format allows librarians to easily input data into spreadsheet format; the pdf format does not allow data manipulation. Does your institution have the ability and staff to use raw data for interpretation and manipulation?

Most important, once the data are retrieved, are they understandable? Is there enough detailed documentation available to help you understand the statistics provided?[21] The vendor's method of collecting usage data is also an important consideration for interpreting the statistics. Can you retrieve information from the vendor's Web site about terminology and process—about how the statistics are collected? Is this process consistent with other vendors? Reports from different vendors are often inconsistent, making it difficult to make comparisons.

To make informed decisions, measures of usage data should be trustworthy, consistent, and comparable with other database products. In the past few years, several initiatives have been undertaken to standardize electronic measures by providing guidelines for assessing networked resources.[22] Vendors can be evaluated according to the guidelines outlined by these initiatives:

- The E-Metrics Project (http://www.arl.org/stats/newmeas/emetrics/index.html) was an effort by Association of Research Libraries (ARL) to identify new standardized measures for evaluating usage of electronic resources and to promote collaboration between database vendors and research libraries.[23]
- The International Coalition of Library Consortia's. December 2001 revision of *Guidelines for Statistical Measures of Usage of Web-Based Information Sources* (http:www.library.yale.edu/consortia/2001webstats.htm) defines mandatory data elements and provides parameters for confidentiality, access, and delivery of usage measures.[24]
- COUNTER (http://www.projectcounter.org/), an international group supported by publishers and library organizations, released its Code of Practice in January 2003, which "specifies the data elements to be measured, definitions of these data elements; usage report content, format, frequency and methods of delivery."[25]

METHODOLOGY

The methodology used for a library's evaluation of aggregator databases will necessarily need to conform to the specific goals of the evaluation project. Although the specific goals of an evaluation project may differ, each analysis is likely to consist of three phases: analysis of user needs, analysis of vendor policies and standards, and determining the extent and quality of full-text coverage provided by the database. At each phase, it is helpful to create worksheets and checklists to track the data you are compiling. This section suggests issues to consider before designing the project and describes the methodologies used in two database comparison projects.

Analysis of User Needs

The first phase lays the groundwork for the evaluation. Questions to consider include the following:

- Is the goal to select a multidisciplinary aggregator database or a discipline-specific one? Are you considering replacing your existing product or purchasing a new one?
- Is the plan to replace current hard copy subscriptions with electronic access or to increase the depth of the collection by creating electronic access to new titles?

For a quantitative analysis of a database, compare the vendor's full-text list to a standard that makes sense for your needs. If the database is multidisciplinary, compare the vendor's list to selected titles from *Magazines for Libraries,* for instance. To assess the database's strength in business periodicals, compare the titles in a standard such as the *Harvard Business School Core Collection* to the vendor's list. To determine how many additional titles you will gain, compare the vendor's full-text list to your library's subscription list.

In 1999, Brier and Lebbin described the title evaluation coverage project at the University of Hawaii–Monoa (UHM).[26] The goal was to compare the title coverage offered by three periodical database vendors to the library's print collection and to evaluate the findings according to collection development principles.

The evaluators retrieved title lists from EBSCOhost Academic Search, Information Access Company's Expanded Academic Index, and UMI's Periodical Abstracts Research II. Using *Magazines for Libraries* as the standard for an undergraduate collection, the evaluators aimed for a qualitative as well as a quantitative analysis. For the purposes of pretesting, they created titles lists from the three vendors, *Magazines for Libraries,* and UHM serial titles and then extracted only those titles beginning with the letter "A." At the end of the evaluation, they were able to assign three discrete values to each database:

1. The *full-text value* reflected the number of full-text titles new to the UHM libraries—that is, not available in the libraries' print collection—that were also listed in *Magazines for Libraries.* Academic Search proved to be the database of choice if the goal was to provide maximum access to new titles. Periodical Abstracts Research II, on the other hand, had a higher number of titles that were both new to the UHM libraries and appeared in *Magazines for Libraries* and therefore was assigned a higher quality ratio.

2. The *abstract value* measured the number of titles owned by the UHM libraries that were abstracted in the database but not available in full text. Again, Academic Search rated highest if the goal was providing the largest number of abstracted titles. However, Expanded Academic Index had a lower number of abstracted titles that were not owned by UHM. Expanded Academic Index, then, was assigned a higher qualitative value for indexing and abstracting a larger number of titles owned by UHM, "minimizing the frustration experienced by users attempting to retrieve articles not owned by UHM Libraries."[27]

3. The *interlibrary loan value* measured the number of titles abstracted in the database and listed in *Magazines for Libraries* but not owned by UHM libraries. The database with the highest number of titles meeting these criteria was considered the most desirable for providing references to high-quality interlibrary loan material.

Although the evaluators did compile valuable data from this project, they also note that the values alone did not indicate a clear winner among the three databases. For example, "Periodical Abstracts Research II had the best full-text value, Expanded Academic Index the best abstract value, and both Periodical Abstracts Research II and Expanded Academic Index had the best ILL value for the UHM Libraries collection."[28] In addition, the authors note that other factors need consideration when deciding on a full-text database, including the library's mission and the needs of the user community. Although abstract value may be a useful measure, for example, it needs to be balanced against the frustration many users experience when they have become accustomed to retrieving the full text of an article.

Analysis of Vendor Policies and Standards

Create a checklist of questions for vendors to determine how closely their product meets your needs. Questions should cover, but are not limited to, the following topics (refer to Evaluating Database Content and Features for a comprehensive discussion of desirable features):

- Indexing standards and practices
- Subject authority
- Search and limiting features
- Extent and quality of online help
- Customer service and technical support
- Patron authentication and remote access
- Pricing

In preparing for the database evaluation project described in Brennan et al.,[29] reference librarians representing all of the libraries in the HELIN consortium held brainstorming sessions to compile a list of questions for vendors. The list was based on features considered necessary for a database and also drew on areas of dissatisfaction with the existing database.

The list became the basis of Table 4.1, Vendor Responses, a checklist used to compare the features offered by the four vendors being evaluated.

Extent of Full-Text Coverage

The database evaluation project described in Brennan et al. examined how closely the online version of a periodical title mirrored the hard copy.[30] It was discovered that none of the four vendors evaluated provided cover-to-cover content in the electronic format. Letters to the editor, book reviews, and brief columns were among the components most frequently missing from the electronic version. Publisher embargoes and deleted articles from freelance authors, a result of the Tasini decision, can further constrain the amount of full text available online. (The Supreme Court ruling in *The New York Times v. Tasini*

TABLE 4.1. Checklist of vendor responses.

Feature	Vendor A	Vendor B	Vendor C	Vendor D
Sources indexed (number of refereed and general titles)				
Journal list available?				
Start date of full-text coverage				
Indexing staff and practices				
Subject authority				
Fields indexed				
Searchable fields				
Subject heading/descriptors displayed?				
Indexing criteria				
How soon are citations and full text loaded after receipt of issue?				
Limiting features				
Fields searched w/ keyword search				
Mark or tag feature?				
Context-sensitive help?				
E-mail capability?				
Tech/customer support (e-mail, toll-free number, 24/7, standard response time?)				
Support for remote access? IP? Proxy?				
Pricing (consortium, FTE [full-time equivalent])				

affirmed the copyright privileges of freelance authors whose works were originally published in periodicals and then licensed to commercial databases. For an overview of how this decision affects libraries, refer to http://www.arl.org/newsltr/217/tasini. html.[31]) A comparison of the online version to the hard copy is particularly critical if you are considering canceling the hard copy subscription when the electronic version becomes available.

The librarians who designed the 1999 database comparison project decided that a page-by-page comparison of a hard copy issue and its electronic counterpart was the only way to determine the extent of the database's full-text coverage. Each of the six libraries in the HELIN consortium selected five journals that their library subscribed to and were also available in full text in each of the vendor's databases. They designed a one-page worksheet, Paper versus Online Journal Comparison (Exhibit 4.1), to guide library staff in their comparisons. The questions on the worksheet combine objective ("What is the date of the most recent online article?") and subjective ("If you were to stop receiving the paper copy of this journal, would the online version be an adequate replacement?") analyses.

At the end of the trial period, the information gathered from the vendor responses, the vendor evaluators, and feedback from the journal comparison worksheets were compiled into a pro and con table for each vendor.

Like Brier and Lebbin, we came to the conclusion that the hard data we had assembled were only a starting point for the complicated decision of selecting a database. Questions and considerations remained: How much full text is enough? Is it too risky to drop a paper subscription and rely on an electronic backfile? If an otherwise quality database lacks a significant feature, such as a thesaurus or subject search capability, do we disqualify it? Although a well-planned methodology yields invaluable information, librarians need to consider usage patterns, patron preferences, accreditation standards, and other intangibles before deciding on a product to purchase.

CONCLUSION

The advent of library materials in electronic format has required collection development departments to create new policies to address the specifics of both the format and the content of electronic materials.

EXHIBIT 4.1. Database Review—Paper versus Online Journal Comparison

I. Date/time of session _____

II. Vendor's database used (circle one):
Vendor A   Vendor B   Vendor C   Vendor D

III. Title, date, and issue of journal (use current issue) _____
_____

IV. Questions to consider:

   1. Does the online version have a table of contents (TOC)?
Yes ___ No ___

   2. If Yes, how does the TOC compare to the paper version?
Same? Major articles only? _____

      Remarks: _____

   3. What is the date of the most recent online article? _____

Note: Can you determine the time elapsed between the time the paper articles are published and they first appear online? _____

   4. How is the journal organized and/or indexed (i.e., by issue, by subject)? _____

   5. Does the online version contain the "special features," such as editorials, columns, or recurring sections, that are found in the paper copy? _____
_____

   6. Consider how the online version deals with full-text articles:

     a. What are the start dates for the following features:

       1. Citations/abstracts _____

       2. Full text _____

       3. Full text w/graphics _____

      Remarks: _____

(continued)

(continued)

    b. Are the online articles really the entire (full) text?
       Yes ___ No ___

    c. How are pictures/tables/graphics treated? _____

    d. When compared to the paper copy, what percentage of the articles are:
       Full text %   Abstract %   Not covered %

V. How easy was it to search for the specific journal and/or articles?_____
_____

VI. Comment on the ease of use for each of the following:

Printing _____

Downloading _____

E-mailing _____

VII. Overall evaluation:

If you were to stop receiving the paper copy of this journal, would the online version be an adequate replacement? Specify yes or no and include comments as needed.

_____
_____

In some cases guidelines applied to more traditional library materials may also apply to electronic materials. However, aggregator databases are a new breed of electronic materials, and policies for their collection must necessarily differ to some extent. Although collection policies may ask the same types of questions for aggregator databases, the means of acquiring answers to those questions can be quite different. As technology continues to change and the library materials take on new formats, collection development personnel must continue to adapt their practices, forms, and procedures to address those changes. A static checklist of questions may no longer fit the bill for adequate evaluation of the library materials of the future.

NOTES

1. Clayton, Peter and G. E. Gorman, *Managing Information Resources in Libraries,* London: Library Association Publishing, 2001; Thornton, Glenda A., "Impact of Electronic Resources on Collection Development, the Roles of Librarians and Library Consortia," *Library Trends* 48(4) (2000): 842-856; Holleman, Curt, "Electronic Resources: Are Basic Criteria for the Selection of Materials Changing?" *Library Trends* 48(4) (2000): 694-710; Metz, Paul, "Principles of Selection for Electronic Resources," *Library Trends* 48(4) (2000): 711-728.

2. Patricia Bril, "Cooperative Collection Development: Progress from Apotheosis to Reality [in the U.S.]," in Clare Jenkins and Mary Morley (eds.), *Collection Management in Academic Libraries* (Burlington, VT: Gower, 1991), pp. 235-258.

3. Yiu-On Li and Shirley Leung, "Computer Cataloguing of Electronic Journals in Unstable Aggregator Databases: The Hong Kong Baptist University Library Experience," *Library Resources and Technical Services* 45(4) (2001): 198-211.

4. Anonymous, "UMI Announces New ProQuest Systems," *Information Today* 7 (July/August) (1990): 22.

5. Cheryl LaGuardia, "CD-Rom Review," *Library Journal* 117 (November 15) (1992): 106.

6. Christopher L. Tomlins, *Wave of the Present: The Scholarly Journal on the Edge of the Internet,* American Council of Learned Societies Occasional Paper No. 43. 1998. Cited March 29, 2004. Available online: http://www.acls.org/op43.htm.

7. John H. D'Arms, "Introduction," in Christopher L. Tomlins, *Wave of the Present: The Scholarly Journal on the Edge of the Internet,* American Council of Learned Societies Occasional Paper No. 43. 1998. Cited March 29, 2004. Available online: http://www.acls.org/op43.htm.

8. Michael O'Malley and Roy Rosenzweig, "Brave New World or Blind Alley? American History on the World Wide Web," *Journal of American History* 84(1) (1997): 136.

9. Vicky Reich and David Rosenthal, "Making Web Publishing Irreversible," in Donnelyn Curtis, Virginia M. Scheschy, and Adolfo R. Tarango (eds.), *Developing and Managing Electronic Journal Collections: A How-to-Do-It Manual for Librarians* (New York: Neal-Schuman Publishers, 2000), p. 19.

10. Tomlins, *Wave of the Present,* p. 6.

11. Ibid., p. 5.

12. Sam Brooks, "Integration of Information Resources and Collection Development Strategy," *Journal of Academic Librarianship* 27(4) (2001): 318.

13. David J. Brier and Vickery Kay Lebbin, "Evaluating Title Coverage of Full-Text Periodical Databases," *Journal of Academic Librarianship* 25(6) (1999): 477.

14. Patricia B. M. Brennan, Joanna Burkhardt, Susan McMullen, and Marla Wallace, "What Does Electronic Full-Text Really Mean? A Comparison of Database Vendors and What They Deliver," *Reference Services Review* 27(2) (1999): 120.

15. Ibid., p. 125.

16. Ibid., pp. 115-116.

17. Julie M. Still and Vibiana Kassabian, "Selecting Full-Text Undergraduate Periodicals Databases," *EContent* 22(6) (1999): 65.

18. Jakob Nielsen, "Ten Usability Heuristics." 1994. Cited October 28, 2003. Available online: http://www.useit.com/papers/heuristic/heuristic_list.html.

19. David Barber, "Full-Text Periodical Databases and Journal Archives: The User Experience," *Library Technology Reports* 36(5) (2000): 19.

20. Wonsik Shim and Charles R. McClure, "Improving Database Vendors' Usage Statistics Reporting Through Collaboration Between Libraries and Vendors," *College & Research Libraries* 63(6) (2002): 502.

21. Ibid., p. 505.

22. Ibid., pp. 502-503.

23. Association of Research Libraries, "E-Metrics: Measures for Electronic Resources." March 23, 2004. Cited April 1, 2004. Available online: http://www.arl.org/stats/newmeas/emetrics/index.html.

24. International Coalition of Library Consortia (ICOLC), "Guidelines for Statistical Measures of Usage of Web-Based Information." December 2001. Cited February 6, 2004. Available online: http://www.library.yale.edu/consortia/2001webstats.htm.

25. Project COUNTER, "Counting Online Usage of Networked Electronic Resources." 2003. Cited February 6, 2004. Available online: http://www.projectcounter.org/.

26. Brier and Lebbin, "Evaluating Title Coverage," pp. 473-478.

27. Ibid., p. 475.

28. Ibid., p. 477.

29. Brennan et al., "What Does Full-Text Mean?" pp. 113-126.

30. Ibid.

31. Association of Research Libraries, "ARL Bimonthly Report 217: Libraries and the Tasini Case." August 2001. Cited April 1, 2004. Available online: http://www.arl.org/newsltr/217/tasini.html.

BIBLIOGRAPHY

Allison, DeeAnn, Beth McNeil, and Signe Swanson. "Database Selection: One Size Does Not Fit All." *College & Research Libraries* 61(1) (2000): 56-63.

American Library Association. Association of College and Research Libraries. College Libraries Section. *Collection Development Policies for College Libraries.* Vol. 11. Chicago: American Library Association, 1989.

Anonymous. "UMI Announces New ProQuest Systems." *Information Today* 7 (July/August) (1990): 22.

Association of Research Libraries. "ARL Bimonthly Report 217: Libraries and the Tasini Case." August 2001. Cited April 1, 2004. Available online: http://www.arl.org/newsltr/217/tasini.html.

Association of Research Libraries. "E-Metrics: Measures for Electronic Resources." March 23, 2004. Cited April 1, 2004. Available online: http://www.arl.org/stats/newmeas/emetrics/index.html.

Barber, David. "Full-Text Periodical Databases and Journal Archives: The User Experience." *Library Technology Reports* 36(5) (2000): 11-40.

Bates, Mary Ellen. "Now They Sell It, Now They Don't." *EContent* 26(4) (2003): 46.

Brennan, Patricia B. M., Joanna M. Burkhardt, Susan McMullen, and Marla Wallace. "What Does Electronic Full-Text Really Mean? A Comparison of Database Vendors and What They Deliver." *Reference Services Review* 27(2) (1999): 113-126.

Brier, David J. and Vickery K. Lebbin. "Evaluating Title Coverage of Full-Text Periodical Databases." *The Journal of Academic Librarianship* 25(6) (1999): 473-478.

Bril, Patricia. "Cooperative Collection Development: Progress from Apotheosis to Reality [in the U.S.]." In Clare Jenkins and Mary Morley (Eds.), *Collection Management in Academic Libraries* (pp. 235-258). Burlington, VT: Gower, 1991.

Brooks, Sam. "Integration of Information Resources and Collection Development Strategy." *Journal of Academic Librarianship* 27(4) (2001): 316-319.

Clayton, Peter and G. E. Gorman. *Managing Information Resources in Libraries.* London: Library Association Publishing, 2001.

D'Arms, John H. "Introduction." In Christopher Tomlins (Ed.), *Wave of the Present: The Scholarly Journal on the Edge of the Internet.* American Council of Learned Societies Occasional Paper No. 43. 1998. Cited March 29, 2004. Available online: http://www.acls.org/op43.htm.

Fulton, Marsha L. "Market Research Aggregators." *Searcher* 11(2) (February 2003): 10-14.

Gregory, Vicki. *Selecting and Managing Electronic Resources: A How-to-Do-It Manual.* New York: Neal-Schuman Publishers, 2000.

Holleman, Curt. "Electronic Resources: Are Basic Criteria for the Selection of Materials Changing?" *Library Trends* 48(4) (2000): 694-710.

International Coalition of Library Consortia (ICOLC). "Guidelines for Statistical Measures of Usage of Web-Based Information." December 2001. Cited February 6, 2004. Available online: http://www.library.yale.edu/consortia/2001webstats. htm.

Kidd, Tony and Lyndsay Rees-Jones. *The Serials Management Handbook: A Practical Guide to Print and Electronic Serials Management.* London: Library Association Publishing, 2000.

Kovacs, Diane. *Building Electronic Library Collections: The Essential Guide to Selection Criteria and Core Subject Collections.* New York: Neal-Schuman Publishers, 2000.

LaGuardia, Cheryl. "CD-Rom Review." *Library Journal* 117(November 15) (1992): 106-108.

Lee, Stuart D. *Electronic Collection Development: A Practical Guide.* New York: Neal-Schuman Publishers, 2002.

Li, Yiu-On and Shirley Leung. "Computer Cataloguing of Electronic Journals in Unstable Aggregator Databases: The Hong Kong Baptist University Library Experience." *Library Resources and Technical Services* 45(4) (2001): 198-211.

Metz, Paul. "Principles of Selection for Electronic Resources." *Library Trends* 48(4) (2000): 711-728.

Nielsen, Jakob. "Ten Usability Heuristics." 1994. Cited October 28, 2003. Available online: http://www.useit.com/papers/heuristic/heuristic_list.html.

Norman, O. Gene. "Impact of Electronic Information Sources on Collection Development: A Survey of Current Practice." *Library Hi Tech* 15(1-2) (1997): 123-132.

Notess, Greg R. "RSS, Aggregators, and Reading the Blog Fantastic." *Online* 26(6) (2002): 52-54.

Okerson, Anne, Yale University Library. "Electronic Collection Development." 2002. Cited March 29, 2004. Available online: http://www.library.yale.edu/~okerson/ecd.html.

O'Malley, Michael and Roy Rosenzweig. "Brave New World or Blind Alley? American History on the World Wide Web." *Journal of American History* 84(1) (1997): 132-155.

Project COUNTER. "Counting Online Usage of Networked Electronic Resources." 2003. Cited February 6, 2004. Available online: http://www.projectcounter.org/.

Reich, Vicky and David Rosenthal. "Making Web Publishing Irreversible." (Draft). In Donnelyn Curtis, Virginia M. Scheschy, and Adolfo R. Tarango (Eds.), *Developing and Managing Electronic Journal Collections: A How-to-Do-It Manual for Librarians.* New York: Neal-Schuman Publishers, 2000, p. 19.

Shim, Wonsik and Charles R. McClure. "Improving Database Vendors' Usage Statistics Reporting Through Collaboration Between Libraries and Vendors." *College & Research Libraries* 63(6) (2002): 499-514.

Still, Julie and Vibiana Kassabian. "Selecting Full-Text Undergraduate Periodicals Databases." *EContent* 22(6) (1999): 57-65.

Thornton, Glenda A. "Impact of Electronic Resources on Collection Development, the Roles of Librarians and Library Consortia." *Library Trends* 48(4) (2000): 842-856.

Tomlins, Christopher L. *Wave of the Present: The Scholarly Journal on the Edge of the Internet.* American Council of Learned Societies Occasional Paper No. 43. 1998. Cited March 29, 2004. Available online: http://www.acls.org/op43.htm.

Chapter 5

Issues on the Selection
of Electronic Resources

Rickey D. Best

Libraries, regardless of size, whether public or private, a member
of the Association of Research Libraries or not, all face the daunting
issue of selecting and funding the purchase of electronic resources.
The issues have become greater since the late 1980s and early 1990s,
when the resources were often compiled on CD-ROMs. Issues relating to ownership versus licensing had not become as prevalent. What
libraries are facing in the early years of the twenty-first century is a
rapidly changing environment. Our traditional purpose of serving as
the "archive" for publications is being altered by electronic journals,
full-text databases, and electronic books. More important, with the
reductions in funding for library support taking place across the country, stronger methods of evaluating the utility of database and electronic journal acquisitions will need to take place in order that we
may better justify our expenditures and maintain the necessary levels
of support for our institutions' curriculum and the research needs of
our students and faculty.

The Auburn University at Montgomery (AUM) Library has attempted to incorporate the necessary support functions to allow for a
logical, reasonable manner of evaluating, recommending, and acquiring electronic resources. The library is also developing measures to
evaluate the utility of those resources in support of the curriculum and
faculty and student research needs. To understand the efforts of the library, an explanation of its history and background is in order.

AUM was established in 1969 as a branch campus of Auburn University. Through the years, the campus received a separate accreditation
from the Southern Association of Colleges and Schools. Throughout

doi:10.1300/5580_05

its existence, the AUM Library had as its responsibility the acquisition of the resources necessary to support the educational and research opportunities available on the Montgomery campus. Current enrollment is 3,737 full-time equivalent students, with 403 graduate students and 3,334 undergraduates. The library holds more than 300,000 monographic titles, has 1,500-plus paper and microfilm serial subscriptions, more than 70 electronic databases, and more than 10,000 audiovisual titles. The library also serves as a regional depository for federal government documents distributed by the Government Printing Office.

FITTING ELECTRONIC RESOURCES INTO YOUR COLLECTION PROFILES

Collection development policies are a common tool in academic libraries. As described by Charles Osburn, library collections exist for specific purposes and support user needs ranging from instructional to research activities to recreational and informational needs. Collection development policies serve "as a guideline for decisions on the selection and retention of materials in specific subjects, to define levels of collection depth and breadth."[1] In a 1986 article, Ross Atkinson identified the primary objective of the collection development policy as "to unify or focus expression concerning the current state and future direction of the collection."[2] Atkinson went on to argue that collection development policies served three functions: referential, describing the current state of the collection, its development, and the desired direction of collecting; generative, serving the selector as a "method or instrument" to transform the collection from its current to its desired condition; and, last but not least, rhetorical, in which the policy "acts as an argument that there is a systematic collection plan in effect, and that such a plan is worth pursuing."[3]

Accepting the premise that collecting policies serve as guidelines to direct the development of the collections, the next question to ask is whether or how the selection of electronic resources should be integrated into and determined by collecting policy statements. Is the selection of electronic resources so different and specialized that decisions need to be guided by a separate policy statement? How do you integrate selection decisions into the collection policy statements, particularly into the conspectus approach?

Kristin Vogel, in her article "Integrating Electronic Resources into Collection Development Policies," argues that

> Collection development policies must be written or revised to include electronic resources as another of the usual formats for collecting. They must not be treated as an add-on to the collection or as an intriguing, but ultimately superfluous addition to the library.[4]

Samuel Demas seconds this notion in his description of how Cornell adapted to the acquisition of electronic resources. Demas noted that the view of Cornell was that it was

> the mission of a research library to include all pertinent information regardless of formats and mechanisms of access, in the mix of resources which constitute our "collections." Given this premise, it seems logical that decisions concerning investments in all forms of information resources should fall under the purview of one comprehensive collection development policy.[5]

Stuart Lee argued that "electronic resources should be considered alongside printed resources . . . and that libraries should formulate an overall 'coherent' collection development policy covering all material." In Lee's view, the policy statement should outline present strengths and weaknesses, identify the user community, recognize the needs to be met by the policy, and be available to anyone involved in the purchasing decisions.[6]

In the AUM Library, the collection development librarian is responsible for working with the individual selectors and the faculty to identify, evaluate, and recommend the selection of electronic resources, the acquisitions and cataloging staffs to ensure that the resources are cataloged as appropriate, and the systems personnel when linkages to the resources need to be created. The decisions relating to additions are made in line with the library's collection development policy statement. Because policies help focus selection decisions on specific subject areas, the issue of whether the materials are electronic or print based pales in significance. As pressure mounts for libraries to move away from the concept of self-sufficiency in terms of collection development, the emphasis on the library as a portal, or a gateway, to information increases. As the electronic materials are selected to support the instructional, informational, and research needs of the campus community, decisions regarding acquisition need to be based upon the institution's collecting policies. The major influence in what to select may be seen in the conspectus model for the library.

Common levels of defining the strength of collections are presented in collecting policies through the use of a conspectus. The two main elements of conspectus definitions have been established by the Research Library Group (RLG) and the Western Library Network (WLN). Each is slightly different from the other in describing levels of strength. For the RLG conspectus, levels are defined from 0 to 5. The definitions of the levels are as follows:

> 0: Out of Scope = The library does not collect in this area.
>
> 1: Minimal Level = Few selections are made in this area.
>
> 2: Basic Information Level = A collection of up-to-date general materials that serve to introduce and define a subject and to indicate the variety of information elsewhere. A basic information collection is not sufficiently intensive to support any courses or independent study in the subject area involved.
>
> 3: Instructional Support Level = A collection that is adequate to support undergraduate and most graduate instruction or sustained independent study.
>
> 4: Research Level = A collection that includes the major published source materials required for dissertations and independent research, including materials containing research reporting new findings, scientific experimental results, and other information useful to researchers.
>
> 5: Comprehensive Level = A collection in which a library endeavors, so far as is reasonably possible, to include all significant works of recorded knowledge in all applicable languages, for a necessarily defined and limited field; the aim, if not the achievement, is exhaustiveness.[7]

To facilitate assessment by libraries, the RLG Conspectus Online was introduced in 1982. Libraries were provided with information for coordinated collection assessment. In 1997, however, the online conspectus was removed from the searchable set of RLG files. The updating of the conspectus was no longer frequent enough to ensure timeliness. The WLN developed software to enable libraries to create and maintain a local collection assessment database for one or more libraries. This service has been in place since the early 1990s.[8]

The collection-level definitions in the WLN conspectus are similar, but a bit more specific, and are valuable for smaller and medium-sized academic libraries. The collection depth indicator definitions for WLN are as follows:

0: Out of Scope = The library does not collect in this area.

1: Minimal Information Level = Collections that support minimal inquiries about this subject and include a very limited collection of general resources.

1a: Minimal Information Level, Uneven Coverage = Few selections and an unsystematic representation of the subject; supports limited, specific service needs; consistently maintained even though coverage is limited.

1b: Minimal Information Level, Focused Coverage = Few selections but a systematic representation of the subject; includes basic authors, some core works, and a spectrum of points of view; consistently maintained.

2: Basic Information Level = Collections that introduce and define a subject; indicate the varieties of information available elsewhere; and support the needs of general library users through the first two years of collection instruction and include a limited collection of general monographs and reference tools, a limited collection of representative general periodicals, and defined access to a limited collection of owned or remotely accessed electronic bibliographic tools, texts, data sets, journals, etc.

2a: Basic Information Level, Introductory = Limited collections of introductory monographs and reference tools that include basic explanatory works, histories of the development of the topic, general works about the field and its important personages, general encyclopedias, periodical indexes, and statistical sources.

2b: Basic Information Level, Advanced = Collections of general periodicals and a broader, more in-depth array of introductory monographs and reference tools that include basic explanatory works, histories of the development of the topic, and general works about the field and its important personages; a broader array of general encyclopedias, periodical indexes, and statistical sources; a limited collection of general periodicals; and defined access to a limited collection of owned or remotely accessed electronic bibliographic tools, texts, data sets, journals, etc.

3: Study or Instructional Support Level = Collections that provide information about a subject in a systematic way but at a level of less than research intensity and support the needs of general library users through college and beginning graduate instruction and include an extensive collection of general monographs and reference works and selected specialized monographs and reference works; an extensive collection of general periodicals and a representative collection of specialized periodicals; limited collections of appropriate materials in languages other than the primary language of the collection and the country; extensive collections of the works of well-known authors and selections from the works of lesser-known authors; and defined access to a broad collection of owned or remotely accessed electronic bibliographic tools, texts, data sets, journals, etc.

3a: Basic Study or Instructional Support Level = Contains resources adequate for imparting and maintaining knowledge about the primary topics of a subject area that include a high percentage of the most important literature or core works in the field; an extensive collection of general monographs and reference works; an extensive collection of general periodicals and indexes/abstracts; other than those in the primary collection language, materials are limited to learning materials for non-native speakers and representative well-known authors in the original language, primarily for language education; and defined access to appropriate electronic resources. This collection supports undergraduate courses, as well as the independent study needs of the life-long learner.

3b: Intermediate Study or Instructional Support Level = Contains resources adequate for imparting and maintaining knowledge about more specialized subject areas that provide more comprehensive coverage of the subject with broader and more in-depth materials and that include a high percentage of the most important literature or core works in the field, including retrospective resources; an extensive collection of general monographs and reference works; an extensive collection of general periodicals and indexes/abstracts; a selection of resources in other languages, including well-known authors in the original language; and defined access to a broad range of specialized electronic resources. This collection supports upper-division undergraduate courses.

3c: Advanced Study or Instructional Support Level = Contains resources adequate for imparting and maintaining knowledge about all aspects of the topic that are more extensive than the intermediate level but less than those needed for doctoral and independent research and include the following: an almost complete collection of core works including significant numbers of retrospective materials and resources, a broader collection of specialized works by lesser-known as well as well-known authors, an extensive collection of general and specialized monographs and reference works, an extensive collection of general and specialized periodicals and indexes/abstracts, a selection of resources in other languages including well-known authors in the original language and a selection of subject-specific materials in appropriate languages, and defined access to a broad range of specialized electronic resources. This collection supports master's degree-level programs as well as other specialized inquiries.

4: Research Level = Collections that contain major published source materials required for doctoral study and independent research include a very extensive collection of general and specialized monographs and reference works, a very extensive collection of general and specialized periodicals, extensive collections of appropriate materials in languages other than the primary language of the country and collection, extensive collections of the works of both well-known and lesser-known authors, and defined access to a very extensive collection of owned or remotely accessed electronic resources, including bibliographic tools, texts, data sets, journals, etc. Older

material is retained and systematically preserved for historical research needs.

5: Comprehensive Level = Collections in a very specifically defined field of knowledge that strive to be exhaustive as far as is
reasonably possible (i.e., special collections) in all applicable
languages and include exhaustive collections of published materials, very extensive manuscript collections, and very extensive collections in all other pertinent formats. Older material is
retained and systematically preserved for historical research
needs. A comprehensive-level collection may serve as a national or international resource.[9]

By defining the levels at which one is collecting, the implications
relating to the decision of whether to acquire electronic resources become clearer. Regardless of whether a library describes its collection
at an RLG level 3 Instructional Support Level or a WLN 3a Basic
Study or Instructional Support Level, the need to consider the acquisition of electronic resources is prevalent to ensure that the library's
collection supports the library's mission. Collection levels have been
fairly well described. The remaining issues regarding electronic resources exist in integrating selection decisions into the collection
policies. As Peggy Johnson has noted, most electronic resource collection development policies are narrative rather than analytical.[10]
Dan Hazen argues that "traditional collection development policies
will not meet our needs. . . . The essential resources are less and less
limited to local holdings and represent increasingly varied formats."[11]
Cheryl LaGuardia and Stella Bentley in their 1992 article "Electronic
Databases: Will Old Collection Development Policies Still Work?"
stated that while existing collection policies were

> not adequate in making decisions about datafiles . . . we should
> accept the inherent value of applying present collection devel-
> opment criteria to the evaluation of whether to acquire a datafile.
> Then we need to add a supplemental set of technology-based
> criteria to the decision process.[12]

The arguments in favor of adding an additional codicil to determine
decision points relating to technology issues are, at present, still in-
fluenced by electronic resources that are available on CD-ROM. The

current technology, which provides access to aggregated full-text databases or electronic journals available through the Internet from publisher sites, should not be evaluated using the same support issues as
for older technologies. Although the need to make decisions relating
to CD-ROMs will remain (especially as more books in the health and
biological sciences are appearing with CD-ROMs as accompanying
parts to the text), the decision points relative to acquiring CD-ROMs
are no longer critical issues. The flexibility of Internet access alters
slightly different decision points that would be addressed in the narrative section of the collection policy.

Sam Demas, Collection Development Librarian at Cornell, points out
correctly that "regardless of the format, the primary selection criteria
are the same. These include subject relevance, intellectual content,
level of presentation, and reputation of the author and publisher."13
White and Crawford describe twelve decision points, which, except
for equipment and technical support issues, would already be covered
in the general narrative section of a traditional collection policy statement. The decision points are as follows:

1. Relevance and use
2. Redundancy
3. Demand
4. Ease of use
5. Availability of use
6. Stability of coverage
7. Longevity
8. Cost
9. Predictability of pricing
10. Equipment—Does the library have the appropriate equipment
    to use the electronic version? If not, what would the cost be of
    acquiring the equipment?
11. Technical support
12. Space—How much space is needed to store and use this infor-
    mation/material?14

Is what you are selecting relevant to the institutional curriculum? Is
the title in question a potentially high-use item that will require multiple
copies? If so, this addresses, in a circuitous route, the issue of availability. Is the title easy to use, or does it require a great deal of mediation

through the library's instructional program and by the librarians at the reference desk? How expensive is the title? Can you afford it, or are there other means of acquiring the information that may be cheaper? If you can afford the title, is it a one-time cost, or will this be an ongoing commitment? If it is ongoing, will you be able to afford the renewal costs in an era of declining resources? How often does the information need to be updated? All of these are relevant questions when evaluating whether to add a title. As White and Crawford have noted, an increasing number of materials are available in both print and electronic formats. In addition to the twelve guidelines, White and Crawford suggest four more to assist in determining whether to chose print or electronic:

1. Information should normally be purchased in only one format to avoid duplication, but this decision should consider cost, use, demand, space requirements, and additional factors;
2. When other factors are equal, the electronic version of the information is preferable because of the increased potential for a variety of uses of the information and growing user familiarity with electronic formats;
3. New information storage and retrieval technologies should be examined thoroughly before the library commits to their purchase and use;
4. When receiving orders from faculty or selectors, requests for electronic materials/information should be treated in the same manner as request for books, periodicals, or standing orders.[15]

Suggestion number two ties directly to the reality that most libraries are faced with: the increasing demand for electronic access to resources at times that are convenient for the users. In the AUM Library, usage patterns for the databases between the hours of 11:00 p.m. and 7:00 a.m. range from 4 to 12 percent of the total for the particular database.

HOW TO CHOOSE

The AUM Library has faced a number of pressures that have led us to move aggressively into leasing access to electronic resources. One of the first pressures was the lack of strength in our journals collections

and our inability to support the graduate-level instruction being offered on our campus. In the university's 1997 self-study, 69 percent
of the teaching faculty evaluated the library's professional journals
collection as being inadequate for graduate-level instruction, and 58
percent believed the overall serials collection was inadequate.[16] As of
January 1997, the library had one aggregator database (Expanded
Academic Index) available through the Internet, along with nine CD-
ROM indexes and abstracts. The recommendations of the visitation
committee for the Southern Association of Colleges and Schools
stressed the need to improve the resources available to support graduate-level instruction. It was determined that the best method to improve access to serials would be to obtain licenses to full-text databases across the disciplines. This would be the least time-consuming
way to improve both the undergraduate and graduate-level collections.
In addition to its one aggregator database, the library had licensed
two additional databases from EBSCO (Academic Search Elite and
Business Source Elite). The university's graduate programs are offered in four schools, business, education, liberal arts, and sciences.
In comparing unique titles held by the library and accessible through
the databases, the library determined it would more than double access to serial titles. Table 5.1 illustrates the additions to titles provided
by the library and the databases.[17]

The decision process for moving to electronic resources was similar to that used by the Drexel University Library, as outlined by Carol
Montgomery and JoAnne Sparks. Like the staff in the AUM Library,

TABLE 5.1. Title additions by school and database.

School	Library Subscriptions	Expanded Academic Database	EBSCO Academic Search Elite	EBSO Business Source Elite	Total
Business	239	149	153	606	1,147
Education	195	32	58	0	285
Liberal arts	361	205	126	0	692
Sciences	284	217	132	0	633
Total	1,079	603	469	606	2,757

Drexel saw the potential of moving to electronic journals as "the fastest, most cost-effective means of improving an inadequate journal collection and a way to make the collection more accessible."[18] Drexel, however, went further by deciding not to maintain backfiles of print journals. At AUM, we determined that, for the present, we would retain print backfiles but, when not required to maintain print subscriptions as a part of a licensing agreement, electronic would be the preferred format for journals. Exceptions included art journals that contained graphical information and color printing and other journals that, because of charts or other access problems, required print for efficient use.

As the AUM Library began adding databases, it became rapidly apparent that additional funding was needed to pay for them. Although the general aggregated databases were useful for less specialized research, they were still inadequate to support specific graduate programs.

BUDGETING FOR ELECTRONIC RESOURCES

As has been noted in the literature, databases are consuming an increasing share of library budgets. Often, the one area with flexibility in the budget is the monographic allocation.[19] Cargill noted in 1987 that

> just as library budgets have had to stretch to meet existing demands for books, periodicals, micro formats, and binding, those same budgets will have to either pay for the new formats by dropping some present commitments, or additional funding must be acquired.[20]

Indeed, this has been the case at institutions such as the University of Utah. Roger Hanson, Director of Libraries at Utah, posed the question of how the budget should be allocated for monographs, serials, and electronic databases. His 1991 article asked "How Should the Tart Be Cut?" Hanson argued that although electronic databases and services were not serials, they should be treated as such "because similar assumptions must be made regarding funding commitments. . . . Now we are seeing the electronic media budget eating away at the serials portion of the budget which in turn impacts on the book budget."[21]

The reality is that the expenditures for electronic resources are eating away at the library's entire budget. From 1998 to 2001, statistics gathered by the Association of College & Research Libraries on expenditures by master's-level institutions indicate that the median value of library materials budgets increased by 35 percent. Monographic expenditures during this period increased from a mean of $120,541 to $142,772, an increase of 18 percent. Serial expenditures rose from a mean $165,683 to $232,559, an increase of 40 percent. Library expenditures on electronic serials and full-text periodicals rose from a mean of $35,149 in 1998 to $88,212 in 2001, an increase of 151 percent. During this period, the mean expenditures on electronic serials as a proportion of library material expenditures increased from 11 percent of the total to 20 percent of the total materials budget.[22] For the AUM Library, our mean expenditures for monographs during this period equaled $304,617, a decrease of 4 percent. The mean for serials expenditures equaled $275,222, an 18 percent increase. The entire materials budget for the library was increased by only 2 percent during the 1998 to 2001 period. Actual expenditures for electronic serial resources for the period went from $20,513 to $138,976, an increase of 578 percent. The proportion of the serials budget spent on electronic resources during the 1998 to 2001 period rose from 9 to 56 percent.

To improve access for our students and faculty, the library needed additional monetary resources. Unfortunately, the state of Alabama fluctuated significantly in its ability to fund higher education. Most education is funded by revenue generated from the state's sales tax; a relatively small portion of funding comes from property taxes. The legislature bases its funding on projections of what will be received in taxes, not on what was actually spent during the previous year. As a result, all of education has been victimized by rosy projections from legislative committees that did not pan out. When it becomes apparent that revenues will not meet funding projections, the governor initiates a process called "proration" that results in a midyear budget reduction for governmental agencies, schools, and colleges. To cope with reduced budgets in mid-year, the only options available to the library have been reductions within the monographic allocation and serials cancellation projects. The worst feature about proration is that when the next year's budget is determined by the legislature, it is often based on the reduced figures following the prorationing of the current year's budget.

To attempt to cope with the vagaries of budgeting, the university in 1997 instituted a technology fee. The fee was $3.00 per credit hour on courses that were identified as making high use of technology. Many of the courses were so designated because of their need for laboratory equipment. After division of the fees to the deans of the schools, and then to the departments in which the courses were located, the vice chancellor for academic affairs retained some funds to support new initiatives that required technology. The library presented proposals to the vice chancellor for funding of specific subject-related databases, such as Engineering Village.

Although this process was quite helpful, it had its drawbacks. The funding was not stable. When it was time for renewals, another application to the vice chancellor had to be prepared. If funds were available, he would support the initiative. There was, however, no guarantee that monies would be available. Efforts to convince the vice chancellor to provide the library with a specific percentage of the technology funds were unsuccessful. Progress toward leasing new electronic resources was either stymied entirely or was handicapped by the amount of available funding in the serials budget. In 1999, education budgets across the state were reduced by 6.2 percent due to lack of revenue coming in to the state. To address the smaller operations and management budget, the library cut 164 serial titles for a savings of $13,418. This cancellation project had a minimal impact on access. Only 38 of the 164 titles cancelled were not available to the current issue in the 33 databases the library subscribed to. Efforts by the library have been directed at minimalizing the impact of serials cancellation by providing access to full-text journal articles through the online databases.

GARNERING UNIVERSITY SUPPORT

In 2000, the university decided to address technological needs on campus in a planned and systematic way. An advisory team was established, the Information Technology Advisory Council (ITAC), and charged with developing a vision statement to guide future technology developments on campus. The dean of the library and the systems librarian were appointed as members and were provided ample opportunity for input into the development of the survey process and the identification of technological needs. The council determined eleven areas for assessment: Planning & Budgeting; Organization; IT Support; Standardization; Campus Infrastructure; Computer Labs; the Library; Classroom Technology; Distance Education & Web-Supported Instruction; Information Management Systems; and the University's Presence on the Web.[23]

After conducting surveys of user opinions about technology on campus and taking a census of the ages and capabilities of the current computers, the ITAC recommended a change in the funding mechanism to support the technological infrastructure of the university. The most significant recommendation was for changing the means of charging technology fees. The proposal was to charge each student $5.00 per credit hour across the board. No longer would fees be tied to specific courses, but it was agreed that for three years the funding allocated to the schools would be based upon the amounts previously generated by their specific courses identified as being technologically oriented. In fall semester of 2001, the change in technology fees was approved by the Auburn University Board of Trustees. Interestingly, the recommendations for spending on technology developed by the council actually predated the completion of the technology plan for the campus. Among the recommendations was to "expand digital access to library materials."[24] In response, the council recommended to the university's Planning and Budget Committee the addition of $75,000 to the library's base budget to support the acquisition of electronic resources.

Of the technological capabilities identified by the council, the one with the most direct application for the library was number 5:

> Faculty teaching and research and student research are facilitated and supported by local, reliable access to electronic library resources and tools, including online databases, digital libraries, electronic journals, and other networked information resources relevant to academic disciplines and the university mission.[25]

While working at the university level to gain support for the library's move to greater electronic resources, efforts were also made at the department level in discussions of access to particular databases. In the summer of 2000, the library was faced with a significant increase in the cost of its access to the ABI/INFORM database. At about the same time, EBSCO launched its new database, Business Source Premiere. The library prepared a spreadsheet listing the specific titles and the availability of full-text articles in each database. The spreadsheet was distributed to the department heads in the School of Business with a memo outlining the costs for each database. The department heads were asked to solicit the input of their faculty on which database to select. The overwhelming opinion was to move to Business Source Premiere. In conducting the analysis, one faculty member had noticed a title that was not available in full text in either database. As the title was deemed essential to the faculty in the Department of Management, he requested that the library pick up a subscription by dropping another print title. The review process educated the faculty in the School of Business about titles in their respective areas and allowed some negotiation for adding new print titles.

MAXIMIZING ACCESS
AND MEASURING USER SATISFACTION

During the ITAC surveys relating to technological support on campus, students were queried about whether the library provided the electronic tools they needed to find information. Broken down by school, students in business, education, and liberal arts were generally satisfied with the library's electronic resources, each with a positive score above 61 percent. Students in the schools of science and nursing, however, were less satisfied. Nursing students reported a 55.56 percent positive evaluation of the library's electronic resources, while students in the sciences, particularly the hard sciences, reported a satisfaction level of 53.73 percent.[26]

To maximize access to journal resources, in the winter of 2001, the library undertook a study to see which print subscriptions were being duplicated by online access. The study indicated that 261 journals were being replicated in electronic databases. Of this number, nineteen titles had embargoed periods, and twenty-nine titles did not have complete full text. Excluding the 48 titles that were available to the current issue in full text, 213 subscriptions were cancelled for a savings of $25,014. In negotiating the cuts, the faculty were offered the choice of either the library cancelling the title and the faculty having the option to get subscriptions to new titles not available in the databases or, if the faculty felt the print editions were critical for their programs, the library retaining the subscriptions in those areas but not acquiring additional titles for that department. The result was that

47 new subscriptions were initiated for a cost of $16,914, a savings of $8,100.

User surveys were undertaken to determine opinions about the library's provision of electronic resources. A survey by the library staff in 1999 had shown that 28 percent of the faculty believed the library's journal collections were below average, and 38 percent believed that the electronic journals were inadequate to support their instruction. An additional 38 percent of the faculty believed that the journals collection as a whole was below average in the areas in which they were conducting research. At this time the library had access to thirty-three databases. The ITAC survey in 2001 showed that user satisfaction with the library's electronic resources had risen to more than 50 percent across all schools. The sciences and nursing schools were the least satisfied users, as reported earlier. In the sciences, the faculty and the students in the biological sciences were particularly vocal regarding the need to improve electronic access to journal materials. An area of special emphasis within the department was ecology because students and faculty frequently worked in the local community on ecological programs. To address the needs of the faculty and the students in biology, an agreement was reached whereby, with support from the technology fee allocations to the library, the library would subscribe to the JSTOR Ecology & Botany collection. In addition, the library would subscribe to Current Contents Connect, an online alerting service for the faculty and students in the discipline.

Support for the School of Nursing was improved by acquisition of the Cumulative Index to Nursing and Allied Health with full text online and the ProQuest Nursing Journals database. These two databases, in addition to their indexing and abstracting functions, provided nursing students with access to 242 unique titles. When combined with the EBSCO Health Source database, which contained 451 unique titles, the library's support for students and faculty investigating health and nursing related topics was significantly improved.[27] Before the databases were added, the library had subscriptions to thirty-six serial titles, twenty of which were unique and not available electronically. The improvement of the collection was essential as the school was developing a proposal for a master's in nursing degree.

The AUM Library benefited as well from efforts within the state to develop a virtual library. For fiscal year 1999-2000, the Alabama state legislature appropriated $3 million for the creation of a virtual library. The Alabama Virtual Library (AVL) was formed with a partnership between the state's publicly supported academic libraries, the public libraries, and the K-12 sector of education. The aim of the virtual library was to provide all students, teachers, and citizens of Alabama with "online access to essential library and information resources."[28] In creating the AVL, the legislature directed the formation of a board to oversee the operations of the project. The board was to consist of three members each from the Alabama Commission on Higher Education, the Alabama Department of Postsecondary Education, the Alabama State Department of Education, the Alabama Public Library Service, and the Alabama Supercomputer Authority, the agency that provided the technical expertise to bring the virtual library to life. The responsibility of the board was to make decisions about the AVL, including selection of and access to the databases.[29] Forty-three databases containing full-text articles were licensed by the board. Of these, four were identified as specifically supporting students at the college level. Ten specifically supported students at the K-12 level, and the remaining twenty-nine full-text databases supported everyone generally. The AVM was implemented during the fall of 2000, and the AUM Library provided additional links on its homepage to those databases in the AVL that were considered college-level resources. Exceptions to this were resources that will assist students in the School of Education in developing lesson plans for the K-12 arena. The total number of electronic databases for the AUM Library was increased to sixty-one at that time. The library has continued to add electronic databases and presently numbers seventy-two.

The addition of links to the AVL databases to the AUM library's homepage facilitated access by the university's students, faculty, and staff to the electronic journals and reports that are available via the AVL databases. By using the AUM Library's proxy server, our patrons are not required to have passwords and are able to authenticate themselves remotely. The AVL resources have extended the journal coverage provided by the AUM Library by more than 3,500 journal and magazine titles.[30] Because of the AVL, AUM has gained access to core lower-division resources that support the university's curriculum at no additional cost. AUM is also able to extend its purchasing power through consortial purchases.

The AUM Library participates in two consortia that engage in the licensing of electronic resources. These consortia are the Southeastern

Library Information Network (SOLINET) and the Network of Alabama Academic Libraries (NAAL). SOLINET membership includes 2,480 libraries from Alabama, Florida, Georgia, Kentucky, Louisiana, Mississippi, North and South Carolina, Tennessee, Virginia, the Virgin Islands, and Puerto Rico. The NAAL consortium includes twenty-nine academic libraries within Alabama institutions that offer graduate-level instruction, of which seven libraries are cooperative members of the consortia. Eight libraries are affiliate members.[31]

Both SOLINET and NAAL support the *International Coalition of Library Consortia (ICOLC) Statement of Current Perspectives and Preferred Practices for the Selection and Purchase of Electronic Media Update No. 1.*[32] Although committed to the ICOLC statement, some members still have questions about the licensing of electronic resources. Notably, Kenneth Frazier has raised objections regarding aggregation of titles. Whereas ICOLC in its "Pricing and Purchasing Models" specifies that "Consortia wish to achieve greater value for their money by purchasing the titles that receive actual use, and by discontinuing purchase of low or unused titles,"[33] neither SOLINET nor NAAL has succeeded in significantly changing publisher licensing agreements for aggregated titles. Despite the objections of Frazier and others to the current licensing models for electronic resources, the consortia help the smaller and midsized libraries expand their journal coverage and thereby increase service for their patrons. Ann Okerson has also noted the potential difficulties provided by licensing aggregated databases in an "all you can eat" model: "If one looks at the rudimentary usage data that the publishers can provide, it becomes clear that the abundant availability of additional materials does not necessarily or always produce abundant new use."[34] However, Dorn and Klemperer point out that aggregations of journals offer libraries a number of benefits, including

> simplicity in the form of a single subscription to maintain, a single license to negotiate, a single access method, and a single payment to a single vendor; to the end user, they offer seamless access in the form of a single user interface, cross journal searching, and, often, transparent reference linking within the aggregation; and, to all, they offer the hope of lower overall costs for access to larger amounts of information.[35]

To be sure, there are drawbacks to the licensing of bundled titles, including the loss of library control over collection development decisions, embargo periods placed on having the electronic version of the journal placed on the database so that it appears well after the paper copy would have, the dropping of coverage of a title without notification to the subscribing libraries, the necessity of paying for access to titles that are rarely used, and questions regarding the archiving of the titles. A major issue for small and midsized academic libraries, however, is the ability to gain proportionately more access to more titles for, relatively speaking, less money than it would cost to subscribe to all of the titles. In examining the titles available to AUM Library patrons in databases to which it subscribes (excluding the AVL databases), the library has gained access to 26,692 unique titles that do not have embargo periods. Even subtracting the library's paper subscriptions (1,549) that are replicated in the databases, the library still gained access to 25,143 additional titles. The value of the expenditures is in line with the comments of Kent Mulliner, who observed, "Now we are paying more and more for dramatically more titles."[36] In the case of the AUM Library, this is certainly true. For example, the subscription cost of $3,150 to the Business Source Premiere database provided access to journals worth more than $335,000.[37] This story was replicated with the addition of each database. The decisions for licensing access to a database revolved around the following points:

- First, did the proposed database provide access to needed titles that were not available in the library presently?
- Second, was the cost reasonable, i.e., was the cost more than twice the cost for simply subscribing to paper editions of the titles the faculty and students needed?
- Third, how current was the access to the titles in the database? Were there publisher embargos of more than six months? If so, are the titles so core to the discipline that the embargo would present an unreasonable strain on our faculty and students?
- Fourth, were usage statistics readily available from the database producer?
- Five, was it probable that the library would be able to sustain the subscription to the database for a minimum of three years?

The three-year period was chosen to complement the library's practice of not subscribing to paper issues unless it could ensure a three-year subscription to the title. We believed this length of time was appropriate to be able to integrate the journal into our library instruction program and to be able to generate usage reports to justify retention at the end of that period.

With the addition of the $75,000 from the university's technology fees, the library spent the following amounts during 2001 through 2003 (projections are included for the 2003-2004 fiscal year):

Category	FY 2001-2002	FY 2002-2003	FY 2003-2004 Projection
University technology fee	$75,000	$75,000	$75,000
Library materials budget	$81,270	$61,030	$67,364
Total	$156,270	$136,030	$142,364

Note that the expenditures during FY 2001-2002 are higher because of the library's subscription to JSTOR and the payment of the capitalization expenses.

As a percentage of the library's materials budget, the expenditure on electronic resources has actually declined from 28 percent in 2001-2002 to 22 percent in 2002-2003. In terms of its allocations of the library's serials budget, the percentage has actually declined during the two years in large part because of the one-time expenditure for JSTOR's capitalization fees. The percentage of the library serials budget expended on electronic resources during 2001-2002 was 56 percent, whereas in 2002-2003 it was 44 percent. Furthermore, of the 26,692 unique titles in library databases that did not have an embargo period, the average price per title during 2002-2003 was $5.09. The question remains, however, as to whether the "right" decisions were made in selecting and adding databases.

Although this discussion has focused upon electronic serial databases, it is important not to forget the value provided by electronic books. The AUM Library has participated in the SOLINET acquisition of Shared Collections 1 through 3 from netLibrary. These collections provide university patrons with access to 36,548 titles (and remote access for students) at an average cost of $3.38 per title. During the 2002-2003 academic year, the electronic books in netLibrary were accessed 1,177 times.[38] Surprisingly, the category with the greatest access was Literature (244), followed closely by Business, Economics and Management (190) and Social Sciences: General (177). Medicine was used 112 times. The initial decision to subscribe to netLibrary's Shared Collection 1, offered through SOLINET, was based on price. With the more than 600 publishers, it allowed our library to acquire access to electronic monographic resources that we thought would (1) match the university's curriculum; (2) improve access for students, many of whom commute and for whom a visit to the library during the week is problematic; and (3) add resources in a cost-effective and efficient manner. Despite the addition of electronic books, the library is not moving away from its traditional role of providing printed works. As Crawford and Gorman have pointed out, the printed book remains the most cost-effective means for storing and transporting information. Paper versus electronic resources is easier to read. Computer screens with the lighting in back easily tire the readers' eyes. More important, I don't feel safe taking a computer into the tub with me, whereas with a good book it is less of a concern. The issues of how the medium of the information is preserved and presented (in printed form, in a micro format, in an electronic format, or some other means yet to be discovered) has been described as being in "a mix that will vary from library to library but only in the rarest of circumstances will involve complete dominance by any one medium of communication."[39]

EVALUATING ELECTRONIC RESOURCES

Futas and Vidor have observed that size,

> although not a qualitative criterion in itself, is one measure of a "good" collection. The theory (and it can be argued to be valid) is that if you buy enough of what is available, some of it is bound to be valuable, albeit surrounded by a lot of dross.[40]

We are left facing the same question we faced decades ago: do the materials we are buying (or, in the electronic environment, leasing) meet the needs of our users?

Anthony Ferguson has argued that

> This is an information-hungry generation, and their needs are very diverse. Consequently, selectors need to put their emphasis on providing access to as much information as possible and leave the decision making of what information is useful or not up to the readers.[41]

Ferguson goes on to argue that in selecting electronic resources, one needs to "emphasize access to a broader range . . . of materials."[42] To provide that broader access, Ferguson suggests purchasing packages of electronic journals and selected articles on demand and consortially purchasing electronic journals and books. Ferguson's arguments are constricted by institutional reality. Does a library have an adequate budget to purchase as broadly as he advocates? While at AUM we have purchased fairly broadly, we have restricted our licensing to those resources that match the instruction offered in the university and provide support for the graduate programs. Have we been successful? Although it may not be the best measure, the library's number of interlibrary loan requests for articles was down 16 percent from 1997-1998 through 2002-2003 in large part because of the availability of the articles electronically through the online databases. Despite the decline in interlibrary loan borrowing, are the exact needs of our users being met?

At the 1999 Charleston Conference, Kim Fisher advocated that librarians "must continue to analyze the content of the [electronic] resource and its relevancy to the user" and to manage the changing evaluation needs with the library. Carole McAdam, of JSTOR, noted the need not to rely on usage statistics alone when evaluating an electronic resource. Chuck Hamaker encouraged librarians to "place statistical assessment into perspective."[43] At UAM, an electronic resource is evaluated before it is acquired. We first determine whether it relates to the university's mission and curriculum and whether access is feasible. If it fills a need within our collecting policies, we then want to know (1) if the resource is being used and (2) if it is being used, that it is providing our users with the value they need. Unfortunately, value is a particularly vague term to our users. With our undergraduates who come in two days before a paper is due (or the night before, in many instances), value is whatever article they can pull up in full text.

As a follow up to our user surveys described earlier, we measured user satisfaction with the library's electronic resources by conducting a LibQual+ Survey during the spring of 2003. On the question dealing with access to electronic information, undergraduates gave the library an adequacy mean score of .23 and graduate students gave a mean score of –.39. The faculty score was even between their perceived mean and the minimum mean scores.[44] In short, the undergraduates were quite happy with the library's electronic resources, the faculty was at least minimally satisfied, but the graduate students were not happy. The library is currently undergoing a review of its support for the graduate programs and will incorporate graduate student feedback in its future plans. While the number of resources available to students should be broad based, as Ferguson argues, ultimately the time will come when decisions need to be made regarding which resources to continue licensing access to and which to let go. These decisions will most likely be made in the same manner as decisions regarding print titles are made: based on title (or, in this case, database) cost, and usage statistics.

How do we define cost? Is it the average cost for access to all of the titles included within the database? Is it the average cost for the number of full-text articles retrieved? How do we factor in the value of article citations and abstracts that are included in the database but are not necessarily available in full text? Dennis Carrigan, in his article "Toward a Theory of Collection Development," states that

> A library collection represents an investment—an asset—and should be seen as such. . . . Viewing a collection as an investment . . . should cause one to ask two important questions: What is the return on investment? And, does the return on the investment appear to be great enough to justify the magnitude of the investment?

A library, Carrigan goes on to say, produces benefits only when its materials are used.[45] Steven Moss, Head of Sales and Marketing, North America, for the Institute of Physics Publishing, noted that usage statistics are meaningful only if placed into context.[46] Moss argued that raw use numbers should not be the focus, but rather use compared with similar journals. Moss also argued for consideration of the impact of the journal, i.e., its use divided by the number of articles published. The approach advocated by Moss works when considering databases with easily retrievable use data by journal title, but what are the critical data? Are they the numbers of titles accessed in a particular subject search, or are they the numbers of full-text articles retrieved by the patron? At AUM Library, 33 percent (555) of the titles with full text in EBSCO's Business Source Premiere database were accessed and articles viewed more than 5 times, enough to meet the interlibrary loan copyright threshold. It is difficult to answer the questions absolutely. Weighting criteria such as those described by Wanda Johnston[47] do not fit with an aggregated database, where selection of specific titles is not possible. To determine relevance of a potential database, one could measure usage. Usage, however, is often impacted by the assistance provided the end user at the reference desk. Librarians who are more familiar with one type of database may prefer it over another equally good or more appropriate database. Usage of specific electronic journals that are covered in multiple databases can also affect the overall usage of a particular database. The AUM Library utilizes Serials Solutions to provide linkages to the library's journal holdings and access to the titles listed in the databases it subscribes to. Users may do a search for the *Journal of Social Psychology* and discover that it is available both in print in the library and electronically through nine separate databases provided by the library and the AVL. The selection of one of the databases over the other will alter the usage statistics of the databases. Without analyzing each database for title-by-title full-text availability, in addition to usage, the ability to assign relevance will remain nebulous at best.

CONCLUSION

Acquiring and making available electronic resources, as Montgomery and Sparks have noted, affect every area of library operations.[48] The increased availability of electronic resources has impacted the library's public services operations as students are not required to come to the library as often to access journal articles. The changeover to electronic reserves at AUM, which began in the fall semester of 2003, has also had a small impact. The electronic reserves program began as a beta test with faculty members from three departments.

The potential effects on library staff are apparent as students move more to electronic access to library resources. Although the issue of access to electronic resources continues to press in upon us, it is important that we remember the history of libraries and their services to their users.

> Libraries exist to acquire, give access to, and safeguard carriers of knowledge and information in all forms and to provide instruction and assistance in the use of collections to which their users have access. In short, libraries exist to give meaning to the continuing human attempt to transcend space and time in the advancement of knowledge and the preservation of culture.[49]

For the humanities and many of the social sciences, libraries exist as a part of the human memory, a laboratory for intellectual experimentation. For the hard sciences, the library is again the memory bank from which to check on past theories and experiments. The need to transcend time and space has been prevalent since humans first put stylus to clay or sketched upon a cave wall. We record images and memories, details of what we have seen and what we have believed, all to mark our presence and to provide our successors on this planet with information that will allow them to understand and to advance in the quality of their existence. The medieval monks, in copying the texts of the gospels, were making and preserving a record of information that they believed was far more important than themselves. What Gutenberg wrought has now been replaced by Microsoft Word (or WordPerfect, or whatever style of communication you use). The changes in scholarly communication are still evolving. Based upon predictions, the introduction of digital object identifiers, digital preservation, and open sources/open standards will impact electronic publishing and retrieval of information.[50] The ease of retrieval and the ability to link to citations from articles will enhance the research process for the end user.

Decisions regarding the selection of electronic resources will remain challenging for libraries into the future. Libraries individually will be forced to address the issues regarding usage and cost of databases and electronic journals. Although the aggregated databases have provided a boon to many libraries, the inability to select specific titles and the average cost per use may soon place the "big deal" beyond the reach of many smaller and midsized academic libraries. The evaluations decisions about electronic resources are necessary to support the educational mission of the institution and will be critical. It is becoming obvious for many small and midsized academic institutions that the ability to acquire all of the electronic resources needed by the campus is not possible. What do we do? First, we rely on access to the appropriate abstracting and indexing tools to assist our faculty and students in locating the resources they need. Second, we continue to rely on the quality of our interlibrary loan services. Third, we continue to develop weighting factors to help us make better, more informed decisions between aggregated databases when our financial conditions force us to chose which one(s) we will maintain. Finally, as we face the need to cancel subscriptions to electronic resources, we must reexamine the decisions that led us to acquire the resource in the first place. The reputations of authors and publishers, the scope and breadth of the content, methods of access, and costs are all elements for consideration.[51]

Although some authors suggest that equipment be considered a part of the overall cost for acquiring electronic resources, the demands of our student bodies have worked to eliminate this as a major area of concern, at least as far as Internet-accessible databases are concerned. The need of students for access to computers for research and for writing papers requires that we provide them with a base level of support in these areas. In most cases, this base level will be the same level as that supported by the university's technology plan. Some considerations should be made, however, if one is receiving CD-ROM files as a part of an archival agreement for a journal. As a smaller or midsized academic library, we recognize that we are limited in our ability to provide access to all of the resources our students and faculty need. As such, we also recognize our inability to serve as an archiving source for most journals. The AUM Library truly serves as a portal for its users to access resources. As Crawford and Gorman have pointed out, libraries need and will continue to serve a dual role by providing strong local collections with access to resources they do not own either through interlibrary loan or document delivery. This balance between local collections and access to external resources will, and must be, based on the needs of the users.[52] Access to electronic resources has changed and will continue to change the nature of libraries in terms of the materials we select and in our daily operations. The nature of libraries, however, has held constant since their beginning.

They exist, in part, as a collective memory of humankind. As the Reverend George Dawson proclaimed at the opening of the Birmingham Free Library, "A great library contains the diary of the human race."[53]

NOTES

1. Osburn, Charles B. "Planning for a University Library Policy on Collection Development." *International Library Review* 9 (April 1997): 210.

2. Atkinson, Ross. "The Language of the Levels: Reflections on the Communication of Collection Development Policy." *College & Research Libraries* 47 (March 1986): 140.

3. Ibid., p. 141.

4. Vogel, Kristin D. "Integrating Electronic Resources into Collection Development Policies." *Collection Management* 21(2) (1996): 70.

5. Demas, Samuel. "Collection Development for the Electronic Library: A Conceptual and Organizational Model." *Library Hi Tech* 12(3) (1994): 71-76, 80.

6. Lee, Stuart D. *Electronic Collection Development: A Practical Guide* (New York: Neal-Schuman, 2002), p. 7.

7. White, Howard D. *Brief Tests of Collection Strength: A Methodology for All Types of Libraries* (Westport, CT: Greenwood Press, 1995), p. 5.

8. Research Libraries Group. *A Brief History of the RLG Conspectus*. Mountain View, CA: Research Libraries Group. Available at http://www.rlg.org/conspechist.html. Last updated September 1997; viewed November 19, 2003.

9. Online Computer Library Center. *Automated Collection Assessment & Analysis Services, OCLC*. Columbus, OH: OCLC. Available at http://www.columbia.edu/cu/lweb/services/col/dev/collection-depth.html. Viewed November 19, 2003.

10. Johnson, Peggy. "Dollars and Sense: Collection Policies for Electronic Resources." *Technicalities* 26(6) (1998): 10-12.

11. Hazen, Dan C. "Collection Development Policies in the Information Age." *College & Research Libraries* 56(1) (1995): 30.

12. LaGuardia, Cheryl and Stella Bentley. "Electronic Databases: Will Old Collection Development Policies Still Work?" *Online* 16(4) (1992): 60-63.

13. Demas, Sam. "Mainstreaming Electronic Formats." *Library Acquisitions: Practice & Theory* 13(3) (1989): 227-232.

14. White, Gary W. and Gregory A. Crawford. "Developing an Electronic Information Resources Collection Development Policy." *Asian Libraries* 6(1-2) (1997): 51-56.

15. Ibid. Republished with permission, Emerald Group Publishing Limited.

16. *Southern Association of Colleges and Schools 1997 Self-Study Report for Auburn University at Montgomery*, 1997: Section IV-71.

17. *Southern Association of Colleges and Schools: Draft First Follow-Up Report Presented to the Special Committee, Appendix A*, 1998: 31.

18. Montgomery, Carol Hansen and JoAnne L. Sparks. "The Transition to an Electronic Journal Collection: Managing the Organizational Changes." *Serials Review* 26(3) (October 2000): 4-18.

19. For a discussion of the impact of electronic resource acquisitions on library budgets, see Lynden, Frederick C. "Budgeting for Collection Development in the

Electronic Environment." *Journal of Library Administration* 28(4) (1999): 37-56; Johnson, "Dollars and Sense"; Withers, Rob. "Not One Size Fits All: Budgeting for and Evaluating Electronic Services: A Report of the ALCTS Acquisition Librarians/Vendors of Library Materials." Discussion Group. *Library Collections, Acquisitions and Technical Services* 23(3) (1999): 354-356; and Rooks, Dana C. "Electronic Serials: Administrative Angst or Answer." *Library Acquisitions: Practice & Theory* 17 (Winter 1993): 449-454.

20. Cargill, Jennifer. "CD-ROM, Databases, and Other New Information Formats: Their Acquisition" in Sul H. Lee (ed.), *Acquisitions, Budgets and Material Costs: Issues and Approaches* (Binghamton, NY: The Haworth Press, 1987), p. 142.

21. Hanson, Roger K. "Budgeting for Monographs, Serials, and Electronic Databases—How Should the Tart Be Cut?" in Sul H. Lee (ed.), *Budgets for Acquisitions: Strategies for Serials, Monographs, and Electronic Formats* (Binghamton, NY: The Haworth Press, 1991), pp. 1-16.

22. The data were taken from the Association of College & Research Libraries Summary Statistics Survey Site for the years 1998, 1999, 2000, and 2001. Available at http://www.virginia.edu/ACRL.

23. Information Technology Advisory Council. *Information Technology Plan: Auburn University at Montgomery,* 2002: 4.

24. Ibid., p. 5.

25. Ibid., p. 22.

26. Ibid., p. 23.

27. Best, Rickey D. *Auburn University at Montgomery Library Assessment of the Nursing Collection to Support the Proposed MSN Degree* (June 2003), pp. 1-2.

28. "About the Alabama Virtual Library." Available at http://www.virtual.lib.al.us/about/index.html. Viewed November 25, 2003.

29. "Press Release: AVL Funded by Legislature (August 1999)." Available at http://www.virtual.lib.al.us/background/funding.html. Viewed November 25, 2003.

30. Alabama Public Library Service. *Annual Report, 1999.* Available from ERIC: Document Number ED 464650.

31. Alabama Commission on Higher Education. *Members and Affiliate Institutions [of NAAL].* Available at http://www.ache.state.al.us/NAAL/members.htm. Viewed November 25, 2003.

32. ICOLC. *International Coalition of Library Consortia (ICOLC) Statement of Current Perspectives and Preferred Practices for the Selection and Purchase of Electronic Media Update No. 1.* Available at http://www.library.yale.edu/consortia/2001currentpractices.htm. January 23, 2003. Reproduced in *Serials Review* 29(1) (Spring 2003): 9-10.

33. Ibid.; Kenneth Frazier. "The Librarian's Dilemma: Contemplating the Costs of 'The Big Deal'." *D-Lib Magazine* 7(3) (2001). Available at http://www.dlib.org.

34. Okerson, Ann. "Is It the Price, or Is It the Pricing Model?" *Serials Review* 29(1) (2003): 4-5.

35. Dorn, Knut and Katharina Klemperer. "E-Journal Aggregation Systems: Only Part of the Big Picture." *Library Collections, Acquisitions, and Technical Services* 26(3) (2001): 307-310.

36. Mulliner, Kent. "The 'Big Deal': I Beg to Differ." *D-Lib Magazine* 7(4) (April 2001). Available at http://www.dlib.org.

37. Data for these calculations used the full-text title list from Business Source Premiere. The prices were checked in EBSCO's *Librarians' Handbook 2002-2003* to determine subscription costs.

38. "Appendix A: 2002-2003 Database Usage." *AUM Library Annual Report, 2002-2003* (2003): 1-11.

39. Crawford, Walt and Michael Gorman. *Future Libraries: Dreams Madness & Reality* (Chicago: American Library Association, 1995), p. 117.

40. Futas, Elizabeth and David L. Vidor. "What Constitutes a 'Good' Collection." *Library Journal* 112 (April 15, 1997): 45-47.

41. Ferguson, Anthony W. "Digital Library Selection: Maximum Access, Not Buying the Best Titles: Libraries Should Become Full-Text Amazon.com's" in Sul H. Lee (ed.), *Research Collections and Digital Information* (Binghamton, NY: The Haworth Press, 2000), p. 28.

42. Ibid., p. 38.

43. Jaque, Diana C. "Evaluating Electronic Resources: Report from the 1999 Charleston Conference." *Library Collections, Acquisitions, and Technical Services* 24(3) (2000): 420-422.

44. Association of Research Libraries/Texas A&M University. *LibQual+ Spring 2003 Survey: Institution Results Auburn University at Montgomery.* (Washington, DC: Association of Research Libraries, 2003), pp. 32, 43, 53.

45. Carrigan, Dennis P. "Toward a Theory of Collection Development." *Library Acquisitions: Practice & Theory* 19(1) (1995): 99-100.

46. Nisonger, Thomas E. "Usage Statistics for the Evaluation of Electronic Resources: Report of a Session at the 1999 ALA Conference." *Library Collections, Acquisitions and Technical Services* 24(2) (2000): 299-302.

47. Johnston, Wanda K. "Periodical Selection Using Weighted Criteria Cost-Benefit Analysis." *Library Administration & Management* 4 (spring 1990): 96-100.

48. Montgomery and Sparks, "Transition to an Electronic Collection."

49. Crawford and Gorman, *Future Libraries*, p. 3.

50. Youngen, Gregory K. "The Impact of Electronic Publishing on Scholarly Communication: A Forum for the Future—A Conference Report. University of Illinois, Urbana Champaign, October 2000." *Library Collections, Acquisitions, and Technical Services* 25(2) (2001): 211-222.

51. Rupp-Serrano, Karen, Sarah Robbins, and Danielle Cain. "Canceling Print Serials in Favor of Electronic: Criteria for Decision Making." *Library Collections, Acquisitions, and Technical Services* 26(4) (2002): 369-378.

52. Crawford and Gorman, *Future Libraries*, pp. 153-154.

53. Stevenson, Burton (ed.). *The Home Book of Quotations Classical & Modern* (New York: Dodd, Mead & Co., 1967), p. 1108.

BIBLIOGRAPHY

Alabama Public Library Service. "Annual Report, 1999." Available from Education Resources Center (ERIC), Document Number ED 464650.

Alabama Virtual Library. "About the Alabama Virtual Library." http://www.virtual.lib.al.us/about/index.html. Viewed November 25, 2003.

Alabama Virtual Library. "Press Release: AVL Funded by Legislature (August 1999)." http://www.virtual.lib.al.us/background/funding.html. Viewed November 25, 2003.

Allen, Bonnie. "E-Books, the Latest Word: Proceedings from the Acquisitions Institute at Timberline Lodge." *Library Collections, Acquisitions, and Technical Services* 25(4) (2001): 469-471.

American Library Association. Reference and Adult Services Division. Collection Development and Evaluation Section. "The Relevance of Collection Development Policies: Definition, Necessity, and Applications." *RQ* 33(1) (1993): 65-74.

Ashcroft, Linda and Colin Langdon. "Electronic Journals and University Library Collections." *Collection Building* 18(3) (1999): 105-113.

Association for Library Collections and Technical Services. Collection Development Librarians of Academic Libraries Discussion Group. "Collecting the EBbook: A Report on the ALCTS/CMDS Collection Development Librarians of Academic Libraries Discussion Group [at the 1999 ALA Conference]." *Library Collections, Acquisitions, and Technical Services* 24(2) (2000): 303-304.

Association of College & Research Libraries. Summary Statistics Survey Site. http://www.virginia.edu/ACRL.

Association of Research Libraries and Texas A&M University. *LibQual+ Spring 2003 Survey: Institution Results Auburn University at Montgomery.* Washington, DC: Association of Research Libraries, 2003.

Atkinson, Ross. "The Language of the Levels: Reflections on the Communication of Collection Development Policy." *College & Research Libraries* 47 (March 1986): 140-149.

Auburn University at Montgomery. Information Technology Advisory Council. "Information Technology Plan: Auburn University at Montgomery," 2002.

Auburn University at Montgomery. "AUM Library Annual Report, 2002-2003."

Best, Rickey D. *Auburn University at Montgomery Library Assessment of the Nursing Collection to Support the Proposed MSN Degree.* June 2003.

Billings, Harold. "Library Collections and Distance Information: New Models of Collection Development for the 21st Century." *Journal of Library Administration* 24(1-2) (1996): 3-17.

Bjoernshauge, Lars. "Consortia Licensing: Implications for Digital Collection Development." *Inspel* 33(2) (1999): 116-121.

Blake, Virgil L.P. and Renee Tjoumas. "The Conspectus Approach to Collection Evaluation: Panacea or False Prophet?" *Collection Management* 18(3-4) (1994): 1-31.

Bullard, Scott R. "Collection Development in the Electronic Age: Selected Papers and Complementary Reports." *Library Acquisitions: Practice & Theory* 13(3) (1989): 209-240.

Campbell, Jerry D. "Academic Library Budgets: Changing the 'Sixty-Forty Split.' " *Library Administration & Management* 3 (spring 1989): 77-79.

Cargill, Jennifer. "CD-ROM, Databases, and Other New Information Formats: Their Acquisition." In Sul H. Lee (ed.), *Acquisitions Budgets and Material*

Costs: Issues and Approaches (pp. 135-144). Binghamton, NY: The Haworth Press, 1987.

Carrigan, Dennis P. "Collection Development—Evaluation." *Journal of Academic Librarianship* 22(4) (1996): 273-278.

Carrigan, Dennis P. "Toward a Theory of Collection Development." *Library Acquisitions: Practice & Theory* 19(1) (1995): 97-106.

Cline, Lynn. "Buying Electronic: The Development of the Electronic Book Market in Academic Libraries—Report of a Session at the 1999 ALA Conference." *Library Collections, Acquisitions, and Technical Services* 24(2) (2000): 312-315.

Crawford, Walt and Michael Gorman. *Future Libraries: Dreams Madness & Reality.* Chicago: American Library Association, 1995.

Davis, Trisha L. "The Evolution of Selection Activities for Electronic Resources." *Library Trends* 45(3) (1997): 391-403.

Demas, Sam. "Collection Development for the Electronic Library: A Conceptual and Organizational Model." *Library Hi Tech* 12(3) (1994): 71-80.

Demas, Sam. "Mainstreaming Electronic Formats." *Library Acquisitions: Practice & Theory* 13(3) (1989): 227-232.

Desmaris, Norman. "Electronic Book and Serial Acquisitions: The Medium Is the Message." *Computers in Libraries* 13(1) (1993): 25-27.

Dickinson, Gail K. *Selection and Evaluation of Electronic Resources.* Englewood, CO: Libraries Unlimited, 1994.

Dorn, Knut and Katharina Klemperer. "E-Journal Aggregation Systems: Only Part of the Big Picture." *Library Collections, Acquisitions, and Technical Services* 26(3) (2002): 307-310.

Dorn, Knut and Katharina Klemperer. "A Subscription Agent's View." *Serials Review* 29(1) (2003): 5-6.

Duranceau, Ellen Finnie. "Beyond Print: Revisioning Serials Acquisitions for the Digital Age." *The Serials Librarian* 33(1-2) (1998): 83-106.

EBSCO Subscription Services. "Librarians' Handbook 2002-2003." Birmingham, AL: EBSCO Information Services Group.

Ferguson, Anthony W. "Digital Library Selection: Maximum Access, Not Buying the Best Titles: Libraries Should Become Full-Text Amazon.com's." In Sul H. Lee (ed.), *Research Collections and Digital Information* (pp. 27-38). Binghamton, NY: The Haworth Press, 2000.

Frazier, Kenneth. "The Librarians' Dilemma: Contemplating the Costs of the 'Big Deal.' " *D-Lib Magazine* 7(3) (2001). http://www.dlib.org/dlib/march01/frazier/03frazier.html.

Futas, Elizabeth and David L. Vidor. "What Constitutes A 'Good' Collection?" *Library Journal* 112 (April 15, 1987): 45-47.

Hanson, Roger K. "Budgeting for Monographs, Serials, and Electronic Databases: How Should the Tart Be Cut?" In Sul H. Lee (ed.), *Budgets for Acquisitions: Strategies for Serials, Monographs, and Electronic Formats* (pp. 1-16). Binghamton, NY: The Haworth Press, 1991.

Hazen, Dan C. "Collection Development Policies in the Information Age." *College & Research Libraries* 56 (Jan. 1995): 29-31.

Hunt, Caroline C. "Technical Services and the Faculty Client in the Digital Age: Presented at the 1994 Charleston Conference." *Library Acquisitions: Practice & Theory* 19(2) (1995): 185-189.

Hunter, Karen. "Going 'Electronic-Only': Early Experiences and Issues." *Journal of Library Administration* 35(3) (2001): 51-65.

International Coalition of Library Consortia (ICOLC). "Statement of Current Perspective and Preferred Practices for the Selection and Purchase of Electronic Information: Update No. 1: New Developments in E-Journal Licensing." *Serials Review* 29(1) (2003): 9-10.

Jaque, Diana C. "Evaluating Electronic Resources: A Report from the 1999 Charleston Conference." *Library Collections, Acquisitions, and Technical Services* 24(3) (2000): 420-422.

Johnson, Peggy. "Dollars and Sense: Collection Policies for Electronic Resources." *Technicalities* 18(6) (1998): 10-12.

Johnson, Peggy. "Dollars and Sense: Managing the Acquisition of Electronic Resources." *Technicalities* 18(2) (1998): 1, 6-8.

Johnson, Peggy and Bonnie MacEwan (eds.). *Virtually Yours: Models for Managing Electronic Resources and Services: Proceedings of the Joint Reference and User Services Association and Association for Library Collections and Technical Services Institute, Chicago, Illinois, October 23-25, 1997.* Chicago: American Library Association, 1999.

Johnston, Wanda K. "Periodical Selection Using Weighted Criteria Cost-Benefit Analysis." *Library Administration & Management* 4 (spring 1990): 96-100.

Kaag, Cindy Stewart. "Collection Development for Online Serials: Who Needs to Do What, and Why, and When." *The Serials Librarian* 33(1-2) (1998): 107-122.

Keating, Lawrence R. II, Christa Easton Reinke, and Judi A. Goodman. "Electronic Journal Subscriptions." *Library Acquisitions: Practice & Theory* 17 (winter 1993): 455-463.

LaGuardia, Cheryl and Stella Bentley. "Electronic Databases: Will Old Collection Development Policies Still Work?" *Online* 16 (July 1992): 60-63.

Landrum, Hollis T. "The Potential of Conjoint Analysis for Measuring Value in Collection Development." *Collection Management* 20(1-2) (1995): 139-147.

Lee, Stuart D. *Electronic Collection Development: A Practical Guide.* New York: Neal-Schuman Publishers, 2002.

Lynden, Frederick C. "Budgeting for Collection Development in the Electronic Environment." *Journal of Library Administration* 28(4) (1999): 37-56.

Montgomery, Carol Hansen and JoAnne L. Sparks. "The Transition to an Electronic Journal Collection: Managing the Organizational Changes." *Serials Review* 26(3) (2000): 4-18.

Mouw, James. "Changing Roles in the Electronic Age—The Library Perspective." *Library Acquisitions: Practice & Theory* 22(1) (1998): 15-21.

Mulliner, Kent. "The 'Big Deal': I Beg to Differ." *D-Lib Magazine* 7(4) (April 2001). http://www.dlib.org.

Nisonger, Thomas E. "Usage Statistics for the Evaluation of Electronic Resources. Report of a Session at the 1999 ALA Conference." *Library Collections, Acquisitions, and Technical Services* 24(2) (2000): 299-302.

OCLC. "Automated Collection Assessment & Analysis Services." http://www.wln.org/products/aca/indicators-cdid.htm. Viewed November 19, 2003.

Okerson, Ann. "Is It the Price, or Is It the Pricing Model?" *Serials Review* 29(1) (spring 2003): 4-5.

Osburn, Charles B. "Planning for a University Library Policy on Collection Development." *International Library Review* 9 (April 1977): 209-224.

Peters, Thomas A. "What's the Big Deal?" *The Journal of Academic Librarianship* 27(4) (2001): 302-304.

Research Libraries Group. "A Brief History of the RLG Conspectus." Available at http://www.rlg.org/conspechist.html. Last updated September 1997; viewed November 19, 2003.

Rice, Patricia Ohl. "From Acquisitions to Access." *Library Acquisitions: Practice & Theory* 14 (1990): 15-21.

Rooks, Dana C. "Electronic Serials: Administrative Angst or Answer." *Library Acquisitions: Practice & Theory* 17 (winter 1993): 449-454.

Rupp-Serrano, Karen, Sarah Robins, and Danielle Cain. "Canceling Print Serials in Favor of Electronic: Criteria for Decision Making." *Library Collections, Acquisitions, and Technical Services* 26(4) (2002): 369-378.

Southern Association of Colleges and Schools. *Draft First Follow-up Report Presented to the Special Committee by Auburn University at Montgomery.* 1998. Decatur, GA.

Southern Association of Colleges and Schools. *1997 Self-Study Report for Auburn University at Montgomery.* 1997. Decatur, GA.

Sprague, Nancy and Mary Beth Chambers. "Full-Text Databases and the Journal Cancellation Process: A Case Study." *Serials Review* 26(3) (2000): 19-31.

Stevenson, Burton. *The Home Book of Quotations: Classical & Modern.* New York: Dodd, Mead & Co., 1967.

Svenningsen, Karen. "An Evaluation Model for Electronic Resources Utilizing Cost Analysis." *The Bottom Line* 11(1) (1998): 18-23.

Tonkery, Dan. "A Middleman's View to ICOLC's 'Update No. 1.' " *Serials Review* 29(1) (2003): 6-8.

Ventress, Alan. "Use Surveys and Collection Analyses: A Prelude to Serials Rationalization." *Library Acquisitions: Practice & Theory* 15(1) (1991): 109-118.

Vogel, Kristin D. "Integrating Electronic Resources into Collection Development Policies." *Collection Management* 21(2) (1996): 65-76.

White, Gary W. and Gregory A. Crawford. "Developing an Electronic Information Resources Collection Development Policy." *Asian Libraries* 6(1-2) (1997): 51-56.

White, Howard D. *Brief Tests of Collection Strength: A Methodology for All Types of Libraries.* Westport, CT: Greenwood Press, 1995.

Withers, Rob. "Not One Size Fits All: Budgeting for and Evaluating Electronic Services: A Report of the ALCTS Acquisition Librarians/Vendors of Library Materials." *Library Collections, Acquisitions, and Technical Services* 23(3) (1999): 354-356.

Wood, Elizabeth J. "At Issue: Dimensions of Seriality in an Electronic World." *Library Acquisitions* 27(4) (1997): 517-519.

Youngen, Gregory K. "The Impact of Electronic Publishing on Scholarly Communication: A Forum for the Future—A Conference Report, University of Illinois, Urbana Champaign, October 2000." *Library Collections, Acquisitions, and Technical Services* 25(2) (2001): 211-222.

Chapter 6

Choosing Virtual Reference Software

Robert Slater
Denise Johnson

INTRODUCTION

Virtual reference services have become increasingly prevalent over the past five years. There are several reasons why libraries have choosen to offer these services. Some libraries noticed a decrease in "in-library" requests for assistance at the reference desk and wanted to provide reference service to patrons accessing library resources over the Internet. Some libraries adopted them to provide "time and place independent" service as part of an overall service quality initiative. Still another rationale was to provide service to home-bound, distant, and visually impaired patrons. Regardless of their motivations, libraries are increasingly offering virtual reference service, and a handful of vendors have appeared with products intended to fill this special need. It is possible to offer virtual reference service utilizing any number of software solutions, as well as products not specifically engineered for library use, and this chapter explores some of these tools.

Generically, a virtual reference tool allows a library to deliver real-time (synchronous) reference service to a user who is not physically at the reference desk. This definition encompasses online tools such as chat messengers as well as phone reference services. E-mail, being a delayed (asynchronous) service, does not strictly qualify. However, the term *virtual reference* has come to mean almost any Internet-delivered reference service, including e-mail and online chat. Libraries planning to offer virtual reference service now have several software packages to choose from. The type of service a library plans to offer will directly affect their software choices. Some libraries begin with

doi:10.1300/5580_06

127

very minimal levels, offering asynchronous service by simply providing librarians' e-mail links or a link to a group account monitored by several librarians. Other libraries want to extend synchronous service to their customers over the Internet, seeking to make the virtual reference service as much like talking to a librarian as possible. Software is available to accommodate the full range of service levels for a wide range of prices, from freeware to thousands of dollars annually.

SERVICE LEVELS

While reviewing the available software options, remember that the cost of the software you use will be a small fraction of your library's overall budget for providing online reference services. Because someone must be available at scheduled times to respond to chat interactions and e-mail queries, the staffing cost of this service will eclipse the cost of the virtual reference tool, even if a full-fledged commercial virtual reference product is used. When choosing a software product, a major consideration is its ease of use for both librarians and patrons. Usable and intuitive software will diminish the need for lengthy training for librarians and make the product more accessible for patrons. If the prerequisites for use are too onerous, or the product too difficult to navigate, you may find that even patrons who want to communicate with a librarian online will not use your service.

Most libraries now offer some form of virtual reference service. The most common method is to put e-mail links on the library's Web page. Most libraries have an existing e-mail server (or service), so this option represents little or no cost to establish. Links often go to individual librarians, which means that messages will be received only when the indicated librarian is available to check his or her e-mail. One step up from individual links are links to a group account that can be checked by any librarian so that questions can be answered as long as librarians are on duty. Adding an e-mail link to an existing library Web page is both simple and low cost, but it does not provide assistance at the time the patron needs it.

Employing chat software to provide synchronous reference assistance addresses the issue of simultaneity. There is a variety of free chat software tools. Some of the most popular providers of these tools are AOL, MSN, Yahoo, and ICQ. The software these companies offer is referred to as a *messenger* or *messaging tool*. If your library chooses to use a messenger to provide virtual reference service, information about the service can be provided on the library's Web page, along with the library's contact information—the username or handle on that service. Although this is a no-cost solution for the library as far as software is concerned, there are several matters to consider before adopting it. First, to use this type of chat/messaging software, both the patron and the librarian must have the same type of chat tool. The tools are downloadable but, in general, they are not interoperable.

Some third-party chat tools, such as Trillian (http://www.cerulean studios.com), aim to interconnect the disparate services. However, each of the major providers (MSN, Yahoo, etc.) is competing to be the dominant messenger service. Each implements frequent upgrades that seem to be specifically designed to disrupt interoperability between platforms in an attempt to edge out competitors. Messenger program sizes range from 3.5 to 6.2 Mb. For a user with a high-speed connection, downloading programs of these sizes poses almost no hurdle in order to connect with a librarian. For a home user with a dial-up modem, however, downloading the same software will take ten to thirty minutes, depending on connection quality and capacity. Even if a patron is willing to download the software, he or she will then be faced with the task of installing it. To install the software, the patron must be using a computer to which he or she has sufficient access (user or administrative privilege) to allow software installation. If a patron is working from a public computer—in another library, computer lab, or Internet café—it is unlikely that he or she will be able to install the product.

Other problems may also be associated with using a messenger service to provide virtual reference service. Messenger services require that users create an account before they can log on and access the tool. The registration process requires users provide a personally identifiable information (the amount varies with the service), which may discourage some patrons from using the virtual reference service. Some messaging services require users to provide a valid e-mail address, which sometimes invites e-mail spamming. Many users, knowing this, will not sign up for any service that requires an e-mail address. Also, each service requires that users create a chat name (or handle) that is unique. As might be expected, all of the most common names have been taken, and some users become frustrated when they have to choose a nonsensical screen name. However, if users are able and willing to overcome the initial hurdles, messenger tools do offer an acceptable level of communication.

All of the popular messenger tools offer downloads usable with current versions of Windows, Macintosh, and Linux operating systems (except MSN). They support multiple-user sessions, so users can be messaged by more than one patron at a time and keep those conversations completely separate. However, they do not provide a convenient way to manage multiple incoming sessions. Each connection opens a new messaging window per session. They will all allow you to send files to one another. If the librarian and patron both have headphones and speakers attached to their computers, the messenger software allows Voice over Internet protocol (VoIP) conversations. However, the quality and responsiveness of a VoIP conversation vary depending on the users' connection speed. MSN and Yahoo also offer video support (if the user has a Web camera), but this is even more bandwidth intensive than VoIP. Although a URL can be cut, copied, and pasted into any of the chat tools, the URL appears as plain text in the chat area. AOL Messenger allows users to send live URLs to one another.

Libraries able to dedicate a library-owned computer to providing virtual reference service may choose Web-based chat room software. A major advantage to this approach is that it does not require the downloading and installation of a chat client by either the librarian or the patron. Web-based chat rooms allow librarians and patrons to post messages to a shared Web page that they can both view and does not require patrons to download special software. There is also no onerous registration/activation step. Software of this type can be obtained from several Web sites (search the www.tucows.com or www.cnet.com sites for products such as ChatAnywhere). However, chat room software is not designed for the type of one-on-one interaction that a patron might expect from a virtual reference service. Chat rooms are meant to be meeting rooms, where many people will be chatting at once. However, if your library is looking for a low-cost way to test live reference service that does not require any downloads or registrations for your patrons, chat room software may be a desirable option. ChatAnywhere (and similar tools) do not require a server-level computer to function and can be run on a very minimal desktop PC. A fixed IP address may be required (or recommended) for the computer running the chat software. Several chat room products are available for free trials, with an eventual one-time purchase price for actual owner-ship/support (ChatAnywhere is currently $199 to buy).

Messengers and chat rooms provide basic live communication tools. Such options, however, lack the sophisticated and useful features you will find in a commercial virtual reference product. To offer a more functional and user-friendly virtual reference service (for librarians and patrons) a library will need to purchase or license access to a chat software tool that has been designed for help desk or reference desk use. These software products, such as the Online Computer Library Center (OCLC) QuestionPoint (the basic package) or LivePerson, provide more features than the freely available chat tools and will host the service for you—alleviating the need for the library to provide a computer/server to host the chat tool. OCLC QuestionPoint (Basic) and LivePerson are both Web-based chat tools that are designed to be used by a reference service staffed by various (and possibly multiple) librarians who need to independently chat with individual users from a large (and possibly simultaneous) pool of potential users. Even these more basic of the commercial chat tools provide extra features that facilitate using chat in a reference setting, such as patron queuing features, e-mail forms for use when no librarian is available for chat reference, databases for storage of questions and answers, question tracking, question assignment, and other administrative features.

Whether you are using a free messaging tool or a Web-based chat software of some type, such services have their limitations. Utilizing messengers or chat room software, it is possible send URLs and other "cut and paste" bits of information, but otherwise there are few advantages to chat reference over traditional telephone reference assistance. A library that wants to offer enhanced virtual reference service—service that will allow librarians to show patrons Web resources rather than just describe them—will want to consider some of the more advanced of the commercial virtual reference desk products. These tools allow a librarian to share a Web-browsing session with patrons, showing them Web resources rather than just discussing them and sending URLs along. Such tools, which might be referred to as *virtual reference desks,* allow the librarian and user to collaboratively browse a library's Web resources or the Web in general. Virtual reference desk software suites were preceded by online support software that was originally targeted for online business, and many generic online help software packages are now available (often referred to as *help desks* or *customer service centers*). Some of the current virtual reference desk tools are actually built on the same code that runs some commercial customer support/help desk applications. However, several vendors specifically tailor their products for the unique needs of libraries, and all feature full cobrowsing. These include the following:

- 24/7 Reference: http://www.247ref.org
- Digi-Net Elibrarian: http://elibrarian.digi-net.com
- Docutek VRLplus: http://www.docutek.com/products/vrlplus/index.html
- OCLC QuestionPoint Full Package: http://www.questionpoint.org
- Tutor.com VR Toolkit (formerly owned by LSSI): http://www.tutor.com

CHARACTERISTICS AND FEATURES

Virtual reference tools are constantly evolving and incorporating new features to provide a better experience for librarians and patrons. When considering the levels of service a virtual reference tool could provide, desirable functions (and cost) listed from low to high would be e-mail (arguably not a virtual reference, because it is not synchronous), chat, page-pushing, cobrowsing (collaborative browsing), application sharing, and Voice and/or Video over IP. When obtained individually (rather than as part of a software package) many of these services are free, including e-mail, chat, and some application sharing. However, if you are seeking greater functionality by having many (or all) of the tools available in one package, you will need to consider licensing a commercial product. Virtual reference tools vary in licensing cost and price structuring but generally range from an initial purchase of $3,000 to $12,000 (which covers setup, training, and the first year's licensing fee) and require an additional annual license fee (which includes ongoing customer support and upgrades) of $1,000 to $7,000. Cost may vary outside of this range depending on the unique needs of your institution. Consortial purchasing can reduce costs considerably.

Many components of the currently available virtual reference tools could prove useful, but the most important are the chat and browsing portions. All virtual reference tools provide a chat feature, and all of the options listed earlier include a collaborative browsing feature.

Most products have integrated additional value-added features. Although virtual reference tools each offer their own unique suites of additional tools, they all offer the following basic features, and any virtual reference desk (or commercially oriented customer support/ help desk substitute) you consider should include the following:

- A chat feature that allows the librarian and patron to communicate in real time
- A browsing feature that allows the patron to see what the librarian is doing (and, ideally, vice versa)
- A way to monitor usage statistics
- A way to handle question assignment and promotion
- A way to accept questions from patrons when the virtual reference desk is not staffed (generally an integrated e-mail tool)
- A contract service through which libraries can hire librarians to cover the virtual reference desk when in-house librarians are not available

These are the most important features of commercial virtual reference tools. Before committing to the purchase of any product, you need to try the features or have them demonstrated for you (or explained, in the case of contract reference librarian coverage). In most cases a user trial will be available and is highly recommended. Until you have actually used virtual reference software, it is difficult to determine which features will be most useful and how well the system will work in your network environment. The components listed earlier will probably be the most commonly used parts of your virtual reference desk, so you will want to ensure they are user friendly and robust.

Chatting

The chat tool is an area where users type their communications and another area where the communications are displayed. Text-based chat tools are fairly common, and the differences between them are negligible. The chat tools offer complimentary features that enable librarians to save frequently used messages (scripts) so that they do not have to type out common answers or queries for every interaction.

The tools also offer customizable greeting and parting messages, further freeing librarians from redundant typing. Companies such as AOL and MSN now offer VoIP services integrated into their chat tool, allowing people to have telephone-style conversations through a chat program. The virtual reference desk vendors have been quick to promise that similar features will be available in future versions of their products.

To use VoIP, both the librarian and the patron must have microphones and speakers on their computers. Also, VoIP is bandwidth intensive and can suffer from pronounced lag times and signal degradation if the connection of either participant is too slow. As VoIP becomes a more common feature of software and Web sites in general, it will become a more important feature of a virtual reference tool. At this point, however, it is still a novelty. There is some interest in VoIP functionality for visually impaired and reading-disabled users. Due to technological compatibility issues, it is unlikely that VoIP will be widely implemented until such time as computers are routinely sold with built-in microphones.

Browsing

The collaborative browsing feature of a virtual reference desk tool is what sets it apart from simple messenger and chat tools. This feature allows the virtual reference participants to share a Web-browsing experience. Several levels of functionality are available through the shared browsing feature of virtual reference tools (sometimes within the same product): page pushing, cobrowsing, and application sharing. The most basic shared browsing experience, page pushing, is actually an escorting rather than a shared browsing feature. Page pushing forces the patron's Web browser to go to a Web page designated by the librarian. Page pushing was the earliest form of shared Web browsing, and it is still available in many of the virtual reference products as a least-common-denominator type of service. Page pushing requires only a very minimal browser, and no plug-ins/downloads (such as a JAVA machine) are required. In the page-pushing scheme, the browsing experience is a one-way street. The librarian clicks on or types in a URL, and the patron sees the Web page in a browser on his or her computer. However, page pushing is more a mechanism for opening a URL for a patron than for sending one as text in a chat session and then having the patron copy and paste it into a browser session. Although the patron can see the same basic Web page as the librarian, the librarian will not necessarily be able to see that the patron has followed a link (unless page pushing is enabled for both the patron and the librarian).

A page-pushing session is similar to reaching over to a live patron's terminal and opening up a Web page or site. The patrons are then free to continue on from there without the librarian knowing when they have navigated away from that page. Consider that the librarian is on page A and clicks a link to go to page B. The patron and librarian both see page B load on their browser. However, should the patron follow a link on page B to page C, the librarian will still be looking at page B (possibly causing some confusion between the librarian and patron). If the librarian at this point follows a link from page B (which the librarian sees now, but the patron has gone off to page C) to page D, the patron will be brought to page D without the librarian ever having seen page C. Page pushing represents, in essence, a one-way form of communication. Although this is a step up from messaging and pushing URLs, it can be frustrating for both the patron and librarian, as it is difficult to ensure that both are on the same page.

Fortunately, page pushing is being supplanted in virtual reference desk products by collaborative browsing (cobrowsing). Cobrowsing allows the patron and librarian to simultaneously interact with the same Web page (or even Web form). Cobrowsing allows libraries to offer remote reference services that more closely approximate live reference interactions than do e-mail, phone, or basic chat reference. It is similar to a librarian sitting at the same terminal as a patron, coaching and taking control of the keyboard or mouse when necessary rather than just occasionally taking the patron to a new Web site. Virtual reference tools that incorporate cobrowsing provide a new venue for reference services by combining online chat with a shared Web-browsing experience.

Full cobrowsing relies on a program running in the background to watch what both the librarian and the patron are doing during their shared Web session. In general, this program (usually a JAVA application/applet) communicates what each user does to an intermediary computer, or proxy, which keeps both users' Web browsers in synch. Anything that happens within either user's browser window is shared. This shared experience is a full two-way form of communication.

When, as in the previous example, the patron leaves page B to go to page C, the librarian is taken there too. In additional, and of particular use with online databases, as a user or librarian fills in form fields, each can see what the other is doing, including filling in text boxes, selecting options from drop-down menus, etc.

Some virtual reference tools also include indicators/highlighters in cobrowse mode to indicate an area of a Web page to the patron that the librarian wishes to point out. This is major boon for those librarians who are seeking to instruct patrons on how to find something rather than just pushing the solution, answer, or result to them. Although true cobrowsing is generally helpful, it does have its own frustrations. A librarian trying to show a patron how to use an index can find himself or herself being dragged away from an area of use every time the patron clicks the mouse. For this reason, cobrowsing functions should have the ability to be turned off on the librarian-side of the session.

There is a level of collaboration that goes beyond even cobrowsing, and that is application sharing. Application sharing (also referred to as *remote control*) allows the librarian or user to take or share control of each other's desktop application (or entire desktop) completely rather than controlling just the content of the browser window. For a librarian showing a patron a proprietary Web product, this circumvents the need to log in to IP-based resources (a necessity in cobrowsed sessions wherein the patron is off site and the product in use authenticates via IP address recognition or password), as the patron is actually "using" the librarian's terminal with the librarian. This also means that the patron can see everything the librarian is doing at the computer, not just the content of the browser. Originally developed as a tool for allowing technical support to manage a remote computer, this is a powerful tool, but one that is not required for virtual reference. The ability to completely remotely control another computer might not be comfortable for some librarians who fear they may negatively affect the setting of another person's computer (or vice versa), a problem unique to application sharing. For an example of remote desktop management, try the freely available RealVNC/WinVNC application (www.realvnc. com).

The cobrowse feature will likely be the most difficult portion of a virtual reference tool to fully evaluate. Various products have problems with certain types of files, and others have problems with certain Web behaviors (frames, redirects, secure sites, etc.). It is important that you test the cobrowse feature of any tool under consideration by using it with the Web sites, services, and Web-delivered databases you use most—especially your library's online public access catalog. If the cobrowse window of a particular product does not work with your Web site, or prominent Web services, then it will function only as an overpriced chat reference tool. When possible, it is useful to talk with librarians currently using the software in a similar library. Most virtual reference software vendors can provide lists of people with whom you can compare notes.

Logging Usage

The ability to monitor usage transparently is a hallmark of all commercial virtual reference tools. Tools for monitoring usage range from the simple logging of activity on the system (and associated tools for formatting this into usable data) to the more robust saving of entire chat transactions. The ability to archive interactions allows librarians to monitor the service patrons are receiving and to harvest these interactions to generate frequently asked question (FAQ)/knowledge base entries. Familiarize yourself with the basic statistical package, and be aware of what portions (if any) of each transaction are saved by default (or what can be saved). If you choose a vendor that offers to save transcripts of interactions, make sure that you know where the data are being saved, what personally identifiable information is stored, as well as who has access to or ownership of the information. If the vendor houses the server and data on their own site, or has access to the data on your local server, you will need to ensure that its privacy policies are in line with your library's policies.

Question Management

Question assignment and promotion are features that allow administrative users to manually or automatically route questions to an appropriate librarian. These tools can be used with both live questions and questions captured by the virtual reference tool when no librarians are logged in. In consortial arrangements, the ability to set up library and librarian profiles can be helpful in conjunction with question management tools to connect subject specialists with patrons.

FAQs

FAQs, or knowledge bases, provide librarians and administrators the ability to transfer a virtual reference transaction (as long as it has been logged and saved) into a publicly accessible database. To be useful, a knowledge base must first be stocked with answers using the virtual reference desk tool (presumably, but not necessarily, based on real virtual reference interactions). It takes time to fill these databases with enough question and answer pairs to be useful to patrons, so even if this feature is included in your virtual reference tool, it likely will not be ready to use out of the box. Some libraries are more interested in knowledge bases than others. Specialized libraries that tend to have repetitive questions are more likely to find a knowledge base of use than are academic libraries, where questions are more likely to be about how to research a subject in the library's resources.

E-Mail

E-mail tools supplied as part of the virtual reference software benefit patrons who try to log on to your virtual reference service at a time when no librarian is online to offer assistance. If you plan to use the included e-mail tool, evaluate its question assignment features. Question assignment features allow an administrative user to preview unanswered questions and to assign them to the appropriate person for follow up. Also ensure that there is some way for a patron to reply to any e-mail that is sent out using the on-board e-mail system—some virtual reference tools use a spoofed e-mail address to generate mail messages that do not allow a patron to reply (e-mail will bounce back to users, sometimes with a clarifying note in the body of the message). Libraries that do not want to use the bundled e-mail need to ensure that the vendor can alter its product so that questions can be appropriately redirected. Managing two separate reference e-mail contact points can be challenging and lead to duplication of effort between the accounts and tools.

Beyond the standard features of a full cobrowsing virtual reference desk, each vendor will offer a number of specialized features. Tutor. com, 24/7 Reference, Docutek, and OCLC each offers a backup reference service for an additional cost. Backup service provides reference librarians to staff your virtual reference desk when your own librarians cannot. Tutor.com and 24/7 offer online meeting rooms for up to twenty people at a time, where participants can chat and share Web pages. Each vendor continues adding features and services to compete in the virtual reference tools market.

TECHNICAL CONSIDERATIONS

All of the tools discussed in this chapter allow the software to be hosted on the vendor's equipment. A few vendors will allow the software, or at least portions of it, to be loaded onto a library server. If local equipment and expertise are available, this option can reduce both the initial and the annual cost of licensing the VR tool. Local hosting also secures ownership of logs and transactions (somewhat alleviating privacy concerns).

It is important to evaluate all virtual reference tools under consideration with as broad a selection of library resources as possible (from the point of view of both the librarian and the user) on multiple computers. Unexpected issues can arise, such as incompatibility with older browsers, with certain JAVA engines, and (often) with a particular database or online library resource (especially in the case of databases that employ framesets, pop-up windows, or unusual file types). Simply having a virtual reference tool that offers cobrowsing does not guarantee that the product will access all the Web resources a librarian or patron needs. In additional, some of the VR tools require patrons to download or install software, which may deter them from using a virtual reference service or may conflict with library or campus computing procedures. All products should be available for trials and should be rigorously tested before purchase. If a different product is preferred, negotiations with the vendor may allow changes to be made that would otherwise require eliminating its product as a candidate tool. In some cases, minor changes can be implemented on the vendor's end that will allow a cobrowsing session to successfully access a particular Web resource.

Some institutional network resources, such as firewalls and security settings, can interfere with the functionality of a virtual reference tool, making it seem as though the software does not work. If any product does not seem functional, accessing it from off site may help the potential customer to determine whether the problem is institutional or with the software. If the software works off site, it may be necessary to have network security administrators work with the software vendor to modify the network's security settings to allow functionality.

APPENDIX: KEY TERMS

When evaluating virtual reference products, you will encounter jargon and terms that are related to Web browsing and programming in general and some that are specific to virtual reference tools. This appendix defines some of these terms, with particular attention to terms used in this chapter.

application sharing: Also referred to as "remote control." This feature allows a person to take (or share) control of another person's computer as if controlling the remote computer's keyboard, mouse, etc.

cobrowsing: Collaborative browsing. This allows (at least) two people to "share" a Web session. If either user in a cobrowse session clicks a link, the other user is also taken to that new page. If one user types data into a form, or selects an option from a menu, the other user sees this as well.

chat: A term applied to the type of program that allows users to communicate one-on-one in real time through text messages. Virtual reference tools allow librarians to chat with the patron while cobrowsing (or page pushing) as well as with other librarians who are currently logged into the system. Some popular chat service providers include Microsoft (MSN Messenger), AOL, Yahoo, and ICQ. Recently, some of these services have begun to include Voice over Internet protocol (VoIP) chat as part of the service.

JAVA: A computer programming language developed by Sun Microsystems that is purported to be system independent and able to run on any machine regardless of its operating system. It has been used heavily to manufacture Web browser-integrated programs (JAVA applets). A program can be developed (in theory) in JAVA and then sent to any computer, be it an Apple, PC, Unix, or Linux. However, in order for this to work, the target computer needs to have a JAVA interpreter installed on it to "interpret" the program. Web browsers have been including some form of JAVA interpreter for several years. JAVA should not be confused with JavaScript, which is a separate and independent scripting language that was based loosely on the JAVA language.

JAVA applets: Programs written in JAVA that run within, or in tandem with, a user's Web browser (or other JAVA-aware application). To run a JAVA applet, a target computer must have a Java Virtual Machine (interpreter) of some kind installed.

JavaScript: A scripting language developed by the Netscape Corporation based loosely on the JAVA programming language. It was intended to allow Web developers to add interactivity to their Web pages. Programs written in this language are "run" by the browser that is being used to view the Web page.

Java Virtual Machine (or Java software): A computer must have a JAVA interpreter installed in order to run a JAVA program. Microsoft released its own interpreter, the Java Virtual Machine (JVM), that, according to the JAVA language owner, Sun Microsystems, damaged the core language irreparably and made JAVA function (or not) in ways it did not intend. A lengthy court battle has lead Microsoft to cease including their JVM in the Explorer browser. The JAVA Runtime Environment is free for downloading at www.java.com/en/download/manual.jsp and is available for Windows.

page pushing: The earliest types of virtual reference that supported "sharing" of Web pages tools relied on this technology. A librarian would navigate to a page and then send that URL to the patron. A program on the patron's computer would then go to that URL. However, this type of virtual reference allows only one-way communication. Librarians can send pages to the patron, but not (generally) vice versa. Patrons cannot see any interactivity a librarian has with a page (i.e., typing in or selecting search parameters on a library catalog or database). Instead, the "results" page is pushed to them after the search has been run. Some virtual reference tools include a page-pushing version as a vestigial feature so that librarians can still connect with patrons who have browsers that are too old to implement newer cobrowsing technologies or that have disabled certain features of their browsers (JAVA or JavaScript).

Voice over Internet protocol (VoIP): This technology uses Internet communications protocols for data (TCP/IP) to transmit voice communication. On a high-speed connection, these transmissions approach being "as good as" regular phone conversations with patrons. However, if either (or both) of the participants is communicating over a dial-up connection, there will be significant transmission delays (as much as five to ten seconds) and poor sound quality.

Chapter 7

Electronic Data Interchange and Vendors: Enhancement of Library Acquisitions Services

Sha Li Zhang
John H. Williams

INTRODUCTION

Technology has been a driving force for improving the efficiency of acquisition in all types of libraries in the United States. Emerging technologies have offered acquisitions managers opportunities and new ways of conducting business with library materials vendors. It is imperative that library acquisitions managers take advantage of technology provided by their materials vendors and integrated library system (ILS) vendors to streamline acquisitions functions.

In his 1995 report on electronic commerce in library acquisitions, David Barber states:

> The Internet is having, and will continue to have, a profound impact on electronic commerce, including online ordering by libraries. It is creating both new ways for existing vendors to sell to libraries and opportunities for new vendors from which libraries buy their books.[1]

Barber is correct in his prediction. Since the mid-1990s, new book sellers such as Amazon.com, armed with its powerful Internet-based technology, have gradually increased their market share of supplying materials to libraries. Through its Internet-based selection, credit card verification, ordering, payment, and confirmation, Amazon.com

doi:10.1300/5580_07

has quickly moved up the list of the library material-supply vendors, if not yet the major one. Several libraries, for instance, Minneapolis Public Library[2] and Champaign Public Library,[3] have placed their wish book lists on their Web sites and made links to Amazon.com. Library donors were asked to purchase books from the wish list and send them to the library. In additional, the Australian National University Library provides a link to Amazon.com's purchasing Web site on their home page. The library serves "as an associate of Amazon.com and receives a five percent referral fee for any order that results from someone linking to Amazon.com from the library's Web pages."[4]

Siddiqui succinctly points out what Internet-based vendors can do for acquisitions:

> Internet has, in fact, become a useful tool that enables acquisitions librarians to obtain required information to decide what is appropriate for collection building; to communicate with one another through communication networks; and to store, retrieve, and manipulate the information, at will and within the laws and statutes of each country (e.g., copyright).[5]

Materials acquisition, like many other library functions, is at a crossroads in an increasingly competitive environment. Acquisitions managers witnessed outsourcing copy cataloging and subscription functions to commercial vendors in the twentieth century, and they should realize that the library's acquisitions function may easily become the vendors' next focus. More then a decade ago, Shirk explored a far-fetched scenario of removing the acquisitions department from the library and making it the responsibility of vendors. Shirk's contemplations were based on five technological trends that were fundamentally changing the way business was conducted[6]:

- Decreasing computer costs as systems performance increases
- Established communication infrastructure and increasing capacity to move data
- Adherence to technological standards (e.g., communication protocols)
- Increasing pool of technically skilled people
- Access to large public and commercial databases

However, because the library acquisitions function is much more complex, especially with increasing electronic acquisitions, a vendor takeover of acquisitions may not happen in the near future. To the contrary, libraries are experiencing more, rather than less, interdependence between vendors and acquisitions departments. This phenomenon will continue for some time.

Interdependence between acquisitions departments and materials vendors has, in recent years, operated in the context where electronic business (e-business) or e-commerce has become prevalent. E-commerce is "the practice of buying and selling products and services over the Internet, utilizing technologies such as Web, electronic data interchange, e-mail, electronic fund transfers, and smart carts."[7] Singh and Waddell summarize the characteristics of e-commerce or e-business:

> E-business is a revolution that brings with it new ways of dealing with customers and business partners, new revenue streams, new ways of processing information, new organization structure, new skill sets, electronic supply chains, new standards and policies, new collaborations and the need for adaptable business strategies.[8]

ELECTRONIC TRANSFER OF BIBLIOGRAPHIC RECORD DATA

More e-business tools are available now than ever before. Mays defines e-business tools as "vendor databases, vendor ordering portals, library system's business-to-business electronic ordering module, and library system's electronic invoicing module."[9] Mays believes these tools maximize efficiency by speeding up ordering and reducing shipping time through use of the library system's electronic ordering module, vendors' ordering Web portals, and e-mailing orders to vendors.[10] However, Mays does not address common protocols and standards that vendors must follow. To access vendor databases, order, invoice, and track, libraries and vendors must use the same or similar data protocols. Vendors must apply industry standards and use devices comparable with the libraries'. Finally, both vendors and libraries must use compatible encryption for tracking electronic transactions. The following are examples:

1. *Standardized data:* Libraries and vendors have long used the U.S. machine-readable cataloging (USMARC) format for their bibliographic records. Many book vendors have even established internal cataloging departments to utilize the Library of Congress USMARC records and to create provisional bibliographic records for their clients in order to facilitate ordering processes. In this way, libraries are able to accomplish their electronic access to titles in vendors' bibliographic record databases, to place orders, to receive invoices, and to complete payments with vendors. Exchanging the acquisitions information electronically with library vendors helps libraries acquire materials in a timely manner. The library may often search the vendors' database remotely for the needed titles, attach the order to the title, and confirm the purchase. The vendor, in turn, can send the records to the library electronically and attach an invoice to the USMARC record for the library.

2. *Comparable data-delivering mechanism:* Book vendors have to work with ILS vendors to facilitate transfer of bibliographic records from vendors' databases to the library's online catalog. Ideally, as soon as these records from materials vendors are exported into the library's ILS, the status of ordered materials should be available to users. To make this procedure work for every library despite different ILSs, it has become increasingly important for materials vendors and for libraries to standardize the delivering mechanism. In a discussion at AUTOACQ-LISTSERV on establishing methods for acquisitions that are usable by libraries, ILS vendors, and publishers, Shelley Neville from Dynix succinctly pointed out that such standardization means that ILS vendors have to address the issue only one time.[11] The ANSI X12 and UN/EDIFACT standards can be used or adapted by the vendor for electronic data interchange (EDI) of purchase order, claims, and invoice data.[12]

3. *Data encryption for tracking transactions:* With the enhanced acquisitions modules implemented in new ILS systems, many libraries have asked that vendors supply additional acquisitions data such as fund codes, pricing, and ordering dates and that these data be encoded in the USMARC record for decoding during loading routines. Although library users may not be interested in these additional data elements in the online public access catalog, acquisitions managers find them useful. With these records,

acquisitions managers can, extract data for the ILS for tracking and reporting purposes. In addition, when a journal subscription vendor supplies its title numbers to the library's ILS, both venders and the library can use EDI technology to process electronic renewals, invoices, claims, and payments for journals.

USMARC RECORD BATCH LOADS

Acquisition information is attached to bibliographic information, and, thus, a fast, accurate, and effective supply of MARC records is desirable. There are several advantages to using vendor-maintained bibliographic databases for MARC record supply to the library ILS:

- Requestor use of vendor-supplied title files effectively batches records by fund assignment and removes the necessity for acquisitions to deal with separates except for purposes of duplicate detection.
- Acquisitions use of vendor bibliographic files and placement of purchasing data, including special instruction, in the 98X field(s) of the USMARC record allows for the automation of both purchase order and invoice creation.
- There is a twenty-four-hour (or less, depending on order options selected) turnaround on the appearance of "on order" status in the online catalog and fund encumbrance in the online ledgers both attached to the correct bibliographic record.
- Shipment processing and invoicing time by the vendor are shortened.
- Problem title notification is facilitated.
- Overlay of pseudobibliographic records or Cataloging in Publication records is facilitated and, to a limited extent, automated.
- Costs of USMARC record supply are fixed rather than variable because of searcher expertise.

The alternative to using vendor MARC records is the ad hoc retrieval of bibliographic records, title by title, from a national utility such as OCLC. This is time consuming in that the same bibliographic data must be reentered in a vendor database for the same title and the relevant purchase order information reentered attached to the separate bibliographic entry in the ILS.

EDI FINANCIAL DATA

EDI places vendor-supplied purchase orders and invoice data (purchase order and invoice number, funding source assignment, etc.) into the library's accounting system. Prior to its implementation, audit trails were made by joining evidence of payment (e.g., agency purchase order, voucher, or copy of a bank check) with a copy of the invoice for materials prepaid or received. Day ledgers noting vendor name, invoice number, payment total, and source of funding (e.g., named endowment fund) were also maintained so that regular reporting could occur throughout the fiscal cycle and balances could be accurately monitored.

The introduction of acquisitions modules into library management systems added to the paper-based system by requiring the establishment of electronic purchase orders to track the disposition of funds prior to expenditure. This amplified the paper day ledger by monitoring not just free balances but also encumbered funds. It also accomplished this enhancement as materials were ordered and transactions were conducted, rather than as a result of a routine summary report produced with an adding machine. Similarly, the electronic disencumbrance of funds and electronic funds expenditure could occur only through the replication of the paper invoice online when materials were received or prepaid. Somebody had to key in the electronic version of the invoice as well as the electronic purchase order. This, too, added to acquisitions workload but was justified as it enhanced real-time reporting of funds disposition. To an extent, offsets to this workload were correctly cited in the elimination of paper order process files and regular manual addition to produce accurate expenditure reports.

EDI has now actualized a real-time savings in acquisitions tasks. The following is a basic outline of how it works in an ideal, sole-sourced environment:

- Orders are tagged in a vendor database.
- The group of tagged titles is searched by acquisitions staff and verified as not duplicates, and fund assignment is confirmed.
- The titles are then re-marked as ordered in the vendor database.
- The following day, the vendor sends USMARC records with library-supplied fund code information for the tagged titles to an FTP (File Transfer Protocol) point where they are programmati-

cally pulled into the library's online catalog, with purchase orders attached according to library-defined criteria.

This begins the established audit trail by accurately encumbering funds against correct titles. In additional, it establishes record "match points" within the USMARC record (e.g., the ISBN or the 98X fields) or the purchase records such that subsequent transactions (usually invoicing) can accurately occur and be matched to the proper item.

For this system to work efficiently with many vendors all of whom supply EDI data (if not USMARC records), protocols must be established in the acquisitions module so that EDI packet transmissions are properly accepted or sent. Figure 7.1 shows an EDI profile for se-

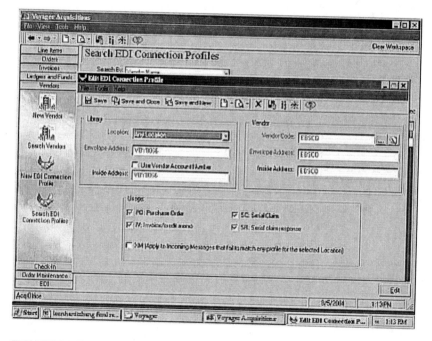

FIGURE 7.1. EDI profile for serials. Connection profiles are security and connection clearances permitting system access and a permissions list indicating which transactions may be conducted by which vendor. In this example, purchase orders, invoices, claims, and claim responses are allowed to a serials vendor using a VOY0066 access code. © Endeavor Information Systems, Inc.

rials from Endeavor's Voyager system that is used for purchase orders, invoices, claims, and claim responses. Figure 7.2 displays a serials invoice that meets the profiles criteria and has been successfully loaded, and Figure 7.3 shows the invoice loaded pending operator approval of the charges. Figure 7.4 shows an invoice for monographic firm orders; the loading proceeds in the same way. However, some line items (individual titles) may load as "unlinked" rather than "pending" because of either purchase order or record ambiguity.

For instance, if an annual for which a serial record exists is ordered irregularly rather than being on standing order, the vendor may "push" a separate USMARC record into the system even though the purchase order is attached to the serial record. The loading program perceives a conflict in that the record the EDI invoice wants to "hit"

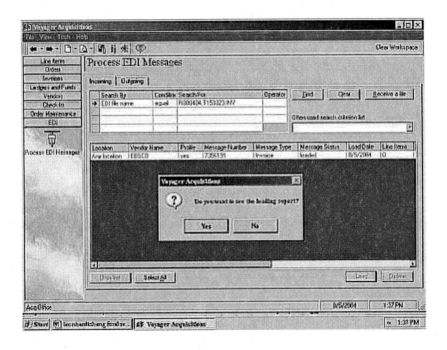

FIGURE 7.2. Serial invoice display. After a packet has been transmitted into the ILS acquisitions module, the operator receives the file, checks the display to see that the formatting is usual for the transmission traffic from the designated vendor, and then loads the transactions. © Endeavor Information Systems, Inc.

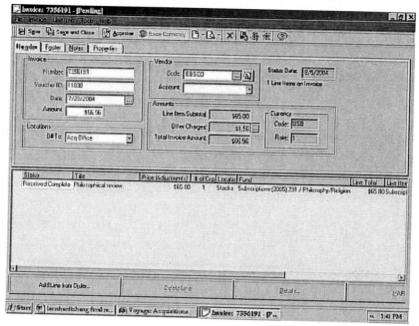

FIGURE 7.3. Loaded invoice pending operator approval. After loading, the document is displayed so that charges may be verified and fund assignment edited as necessary. The document can then be approved. © Endeavor Information Systems, Inc.

has no purchase order attached. Therefore, the invoice line item loads "unlinked."

With this initial push/pull EDI setup, invoicing is then automatic. Items ordered in a session may come as a batch (see Figure 7.4) or piecemeal (see Figure 7.3) at some future date, the match points in the bibliographic record or purchase order affording the link between the invoice and the individual items. Figure 7.5 indicates the "match points" placement in a Voyager serial record. Through such match points, the USMARC record, the electronic purchase order, and the electronic invoice are all linked together. Thus, when the invoice is approved as part of the physical receiving process for a monograph, the electronic expenditure of funds on the invoice electronically disencumbers the funds on the electronic purchase order. In this way, ac-

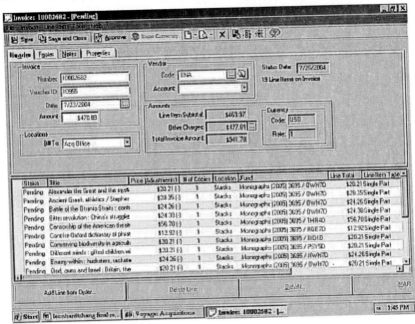

FIGURE 7.4. A monograph firm order invoice to compare with the serial invoice shown in Figure 7.3. Any ambiguity in purchase order assignment or match points will cause a line item (title) to load unlinked, forcing the operator to manually relink before the invoice can be processed. © Endeavor Information Systems, Inc.

tual, real-time fiscal tracking of encumbrances and expenditures and actual savings of acquisitions workload occur.

In an ideal situation, EDI represents substantial savings in time for the electronic replication of a traditional audit trail. However, most acquisitions departments do not stop maintaining a paper-based records system, some just as elaborate as those from prior decades. To an extent, this dual system maintenance is the result of caution, administrative requirements, or a cumbersome interface between a new, library accounting module and an old, agency controller system. However, it is also the result of an intermediate stage in the effort to standardize the rules of electronic commerce successfully at the national and international levels.

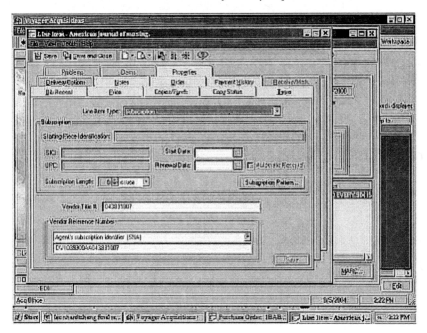

FIGURE 7.5. A line item detail screen that shows the placement of match points in the bottom three fields. These match points may be keyed in or scanned in from barcode inventory lists. Newer versions of ILS software allow the vendor to programmatically change these match point identifiers automatically, over time. © Endeavor Information Systems, Inc.

CONCLUSION

FTP USMARC record bulk loads in conjunction with the EDI transmission of invoice data have made a profound change in acquisitions management. Efficiencies such as real-time encumbrance of funds and twenty-four-hour appearance of "on order" status in the OPAC have facilitated the orderly and timely conduct of materials expenditure. Both ANSI X12 and UN/EDIFACT standards are ongoing works rather than static and transitory models. However, the mere prospect of ongoing changes in these already efficiently applied standards should be a cause for some concern. UN/EDIFACT currently has thirty messages in development.[13] ANSI X12 currently has eight subsections in draft or review.[14] Although ILS and materials vendors employ relatively few of the available transaction sets, it is conceivable that newly modified standards will impact library acquisitions work.

EDI has produced an inflexible interdependence between libraries and vendor technical services: library acquisitions units have downsized after implementation of EDI invoicing and claiming, which has, in turn, forced vendors to strictly comply with the technical requirements of supplying acquisitions metadata in addition to library materials. The complexity of establishing successful EDI subroutines and linking these routines makes the prospect for further change unattractive, to say the least, if those changes and every conceivable impact are not carefully and thoroughly thought out prior to their implementation.

NOTES

1. David Barber, "Electronic Commerce in Library Acquisitions with the Survey of Bookseller and Subscription Agency Services," *Library Technology Reports* 31(5), 1995: 513.

2. Minneapolis Public Library, "Our Wish List for Book Donations," http://www.mplib.org/wishlist.asp. Accessed July 26, 2004.

3. Champaign Public Library Foundation, "Buy a Book for the Library at Amazon.com," http://www.champaign.org/support/fn_amazon_wishlist.html. Accessed July 26, 2004.

4. Australian National University Library, "Obtain an Item: Self Service Book—Amazon.com," http://anulib.anu.edu.au/docdel/obtain/diy_book.html.

5. Moid A. Siddiqui, "Management for Change in Acquisitions in Academic Libraries," *The Electronic Library* 21(4), 2003: 352.

6. Gary M. Shirk, "Contract Acquisitions: Change, Technology, and the New Library Vendor Partnership," *Library Acquisitions: Practice & Theory* 17(2), 1993: 145-153.

7. "What is e-commerce?" http://www.ilr.cornell.edu/library/subjectGuides/ecommerce.html.

8. Mohini Singh and Dianne Waddell, *E-Business Innovation and Change Management* (London: Idea Group Publishing, 2004), p. vi.

9. Antje Mays, "Biz of Acq—Using Technology to Increase Collaboration Between the Library, Technical Faculty, and the Campus at Large," *Against the Grain,* November 2003: 74.

10. Ibid., p. 76.

11. Shelley Neville, "Vendor's Perspective," e-mail to AUTOACQ=L@Listserv.nd.edu. Accessed September 26, 2003.

12. The X12 standard(s) have been under development for twenty-seven years, and are composed of more than 300 transaction sets that offer parameters for most normal business transactions. An overview of these sets is available at http://www.x12.org/. Similarly, the United Nations' standards for Electronic Data Interchange for Admin-

istration, Commerce and Transport (UN/EDIFACT) offer guidelines for international business transactions and also have a twenty-seven-year history of ongoing development. An overview of these is available at http://www.unece.org/trade/untdid/texts/d100_d.htm.

13. UN/CEFACT, "Messages in Development," http://www.unece.org/trade/untdid/mid/index.htm. Accessed August 5, 2004.

14. Accredited Standards Committee (ASC) X12, "Standards Development," http://www.disa.org/x12org/subcommittees/dev/dpANS_V5.cfm. Accessed August 5, 2004.

Index

Page numbers followed by the letter "f" indicate figures; those followed by the letter "t" indicate tables.

Order a copy of this book with this form or online at:
http://www.haworthpress.com/store/product.asp?sku=5580

HANDBOOK OF ELECTRONIC AND DIGITAL ACQUISITIONS

_____ in hardbound at $34.95 (ISBN-13: 978-0-7890-2291-2; ISBN-10: 0-7890-2291-5)

_____ in softbound at $24.95 (ISBN-13: 978-0-7890-2292-9; ISBN-10: 0-7890-2292-3)

Or order online and use special offer code HEC25 in the shopping cart.

COST OF BOOKS_____

POSTAGE & HANDLING_____
(US: $4.00 for first book & $1.50
for each additional book)
(Outside US: $5.00 for first book
& $2.00 for each additional book)

SUBTOTAL_____

IN CANADA: ADD 7% GST_____

STATE TAX_____
(NJ, NY, OH, MN, CA, IL, IN, PA, & SD
residents, add appropriate local sales tax)

FINAL TOTAL_____
(If paying in Canadian funds,
convert using the current
exchange rate, UNESCO
coupons welcome)

☐ **BILL ME LATER:** (Bill-me option is good on US/Canada/Mexico orders only; not good to jobbers, wholesalers, or subscription agencies.)

☐ Check here if billing address is different from shipping address and attach purchase order and billing address information.

Signature_____

☐ **PAYMENT ENCLOSED: $**_____

☐ **PLEASE CHARGE TO MY CREDIT CARD.**

☐ Visa ☐ MasterCard ☐ AmEx ☐ Discover
☐ Diner's Club ☐ Eurocard ☐ JCB

Account #_____

Exp. Date_____

Signature_____

Prices in US dollars and subject to change without notice.

NAME_____
INSTITUTION_____
ADDRESS_____
CITY_____
STATE/ZIP_____
COUNTRY_____ COUNTY (NY residents only)_____
TEL_____ FAX_____
E-MAIL_____

May we use your e-mail address for confirmations and other types of information? ☐ Yes ☐ No
We appreciate receiving your e-mail address and fax number. Haworth would like to e-mail or fax special discount offers to you, as a preferred customer. **We will never share, rent, or exchange your e-mail address or fax number.** We regard such actions as an invasion of your privacy.

Order From Your Local Bookstore or Directly From
The Haworth Press, Inc.
10 Alice Street, Binghamton, New York 13904-1580 • USA
TELEPHONE: 1-800-HAWORTH (1-800-429-6784) / Outside US/Canada: (607) 722-5857
FAX: 1-800-895-0582 / Outside US/Canada: (607) 771-0012
E-mail to: orders@haworthpress.com

For orders outside US and Canada, you may wish to order through your local
sales representative, distributor, or bookseller.
For information, see http://haworthpress.com/distributors

(Discounts are available for individual orders in US and Canada only, not booksellers/distributors.)
PLEASE PHOTOCOPY THIS FORM FOR YOUR PERSONAL USE.
http://www.HaworthPress.com   BOF06